WORSHIP PROGRAMS IN THE FINE ARTS FOR YOUNG PEOPLE

THE NAZARENE, by Henry Stanley Todd

WORSHIP PROGRAMS
IN THE
FINE ARTS
FOR YOUNG PEOPLE

By
ALICE ANDERSON BAYS

ABINGDON-COKESBURY PRESS

NEW YORK ⚫ NASHVILLE

WORSHIP PROGRAMS IN THE FINE ARTS
FOR YOUNG PEOPLE
COPYRIGHT, MCMXL
By WHITMORE & SMITH

K

PRINTED IN THE UNITED STATES OF AMERICA

TO MY HUSBAND

FOREWORD

THAT YOUNG PEOPLE may be led to know God, to understand his purposes, and to commit themselves to his will is the aim of this book. In a former volume, WORSHIP PROGRAMS AND STORIES, the writer attempted to illustrate ways in which stories may be used to lead young people into a more vital relationship with God and into more Christian ways of living. Stories chosen from various sources were the center around which the worship services were built. In the present volume, instead of using stories from literature, the author chose selections from the fine arts—painting, sculpture, and music. Around each is built a worship service which is designed to lead to a clearer understanding of the message contained in the work of art.

This book has grown out of a desire to share with others material which has enriched worship in young people's groups in local churches, in colleges, in camps, and in summer conferences. Although these services were planned with the needs of young people in mind, with slight variation they may be adapted to other groups. If a more formal program is desired, an anthem may be used instead of a hymn; if a simple service is desired, certain parts of the program may be omitted. Regardless of the size of the group or the physical equipment, the material should be adapted to the needs of the worshipers, and every detail of the program should be mastered if the worship is to be made meaningful.

These programs have grown out of actual experience in leading young people's worship services in the church attended by the writer, and have also been used by a number of other groups in the smaller as well as in the larger churches. They are not sent out as model services or set programs to follow, but as illustrations of ways in which the fine arts may be used to enrich worship. Care has been used in selecting Scripture, prayers, poems, and hymns which will provide young people with appropriate language of worship. The ideas expressed have been carefully studied to determine whether they are within the range of experience of the group.

The writer wishes to express her sincere appreciation to the young people who have shared in the development of these programs, to Elizabeth Wray Taylor for her critically helpful comments, to Blanche Duncan Wells for reading the manuscript and for literary criticism. Grateful acknowledgment is made to authors as well as to publishers who have granted permission to use copyright material. Every effort has been made to determine authorship, to trace ownership of all copyright material, and to give proper credit. The writer is not conscious of any infringement directly or indirectly; but should there be any question regarding the use of any material, the author will take pleasure in making proper acknowledgment in future editions.

This book is sent out with the earnest hope that through the use of the programs, worship may be enriched and young people may be led into a more meaningful fellowship with God and into a desire to co-operate with his purposes.

ALICE ANDERSON BAYS

Kingsport, Tennessee

CONTENTS

PART THREE

HYMNS

APPENDIX

ILLUSTRATIONS

INTRODUCTION

To LEAD YOUNG PEOPLE into worship experiences which will have possibilities of real spiritual growth, the program must be related to the actual ongoing experiences of the group. The planned program of worship is only a part of the total worship experience and should be supplemented with worship in the home and with the entire congregation. There should be provided in the daily routine many opportunities for fellowship with persons to whom God is real, and also a chance to share in the real work of the church. Worship takes on added significance when young people have the privilege of fellowship with persons who are striving to co-operate with God. It is too much to expect a brief worship service to provide a medium of expression for the longings and aspirations of growing persons, to clarify their religious ideas, and to give direction to their lives. But a total worship experience will tend to bring about these results.

It seems that the writer of Psalm 122 had in mind a complete worship experience when he said, "I was glad when they said unto me, Let us go into the house of the Lord." He spoke first of the joy he felt in worship; but, instead of stopping with the emotional uplift, he went on to creative expression, to new decisions, and closed with, "I will seek thy good." If the worshiper is content to stop with the first step, with rejoicing in the presence of God, it may be that nothing else will happen to him. But when worship has fruited, one goes from inspiration to a definite commitment of life to God's will and purpose.

It is comparatively easy for adult leaders to talk about God, but it is more difficult to lead a group of early adolescents to achieve an experience of worship. It takes time to lead to a sense of the reality of God, to understand the way God works and to bring about changed attitudes. Such an opportunity may be found on the occasion of a trip to the country or during a walk in a park, provided there is sufficient time to explore the wonders of the universe, and an effort is made to lead the worshipers to stand in adoration in the presence of God as revealed in nature. High moments of worship are the results which one may expect from such fellowship.

In the midst of ordinary activities, one may suddenly come face to face with the Creator, and relationships may be lifted to a higher level. For example, a twelve-year-old boy, upon locating the tracks of a prehistoric animal, remarked to the adult accompanying him, "Just think, we are reading written on stone the history of some of the earliest animals." Following this experience it was not difficult to lead him to an understanding of God's providence in an orderly and continuous process of creation.

To use this volume creatively would be to refer to it as a source book for material to enrich and vary worship experiences.. Certain programs have been developed with the needs of the Intermediates in mind, but with adaptation all of the services are usable with this group. It will help when using a program based upon the message of a painting or a statue to have a good reproduction of the work of art placed where it can be seen by the worshipers. The picture may also be thrown upon a screen, or a small print may be attached to the printed program. Reproductions of most of the paintings and pictures of most of the statues may be secured from the various denominational headquarters. If this source cannot supply them, a list of the art companies from whom they may be secured will be found in the appendix.

The following books will be helpful to those who desire to do a creative piece of work in building other programs on this theme:

Albert Edward Bailey, *The Gospel in Art,* Pilgrim Press
Albert Edward Bailey, *Art and Education,* Abingdon Press
Cynthia Pearl Maus, *Christ and the Fine Arts,* Harper Brothers
Daniel Johnson Fleming, *Each in His Own Brush,* Friendship Press
Charles L. Barstow, *Famous Sculpture,* D. Appleton-Century Company
Edwin Rayner, *Famous Statues,* Grossett & Dunlap
Augustine Smith, *Lyric Religion,* D. Appleton-Century Company
Charles C. Washburn, *Hymn Interpretations,* Cokesbury Press
Robert Guy McCutcheon, *Our Hymnody,* Abingdon Press
Cecile Rudin, *Stories of Hymns We Love,* Rudin, John & Company
Louis F. Benson, *Studies of Familiar Hymns,* Westminster Press

Fleming says, "Art has always been the handmaid of religion, and in turn, religion has been the creator and preserver of art." The masterpieces of art contain a vast storehouse of truth for those who are willing to set aside the daily routine and take time to receive the message. The artist is an interpreter; he has something to say, and he conveys his message by means of lines, colors, lights, shadows, and symbols. In his attempt to open up new avenues of appreciation he helps us to discover beauty and truth in unaccustomed forms. Instead of revealing his entire message, he may show only one angle of the truth and trust that eventually we will be led into possession of the entire truth.

Since music is the language of worship, it is possible through the use of music to prepare the group for worship and to provide a medium for the expression of certain vague longings and aspirations. It also strengthens our desires for Christian living and stimulates an interest in serving others. In using the programs, if the tune is unfamiliar to the group, the lines of the hymn may be read as a poem, or a familiar tune of the same meter may be substituted. By referring to the metrical index in the hymnal, other hymns of the same meter may be located and one may be substituted in which the tempo of the music harmonizes with the message of the hymn. For example, the words of "Once to Every Man and Nation" may be sung to the tune of "Austrian Hymn."

Christ sang a song with his disciples and went from the Last Supper to Gethsemane. St. Paul advises, "Let the words of Christ dwell in you richly; in all wisdom teaching and admonishing one another with psalms and hymns and spiritual songs." Some of our hymns are paraphrases of the Psalms, which the people of God have sung through the ages. When we use music in worship we are continuing a custom which worshipers have found valuable from the earliest times.

PART ONE

PAINTINGS

SERVICE 1

THE NAZARENE

(*Henry Stanley Todd*)

AIM: To lead to a realization that through prayer we have the same privilege of companionship with Christ as did the disciples in the days of his flesh.

PRELUDE: Hymn tune "Crusader's Hymn."

CALL TO WORSHIP:

O come, let us worship and bow down; let us kneel before the Lord and call upon his name.

We will bless the Lord at all times; we will worship him in the beauty of holiness, and magnify his name together.

PRAYER:

Look upon us, O Lord, and let all the darkness of our souls vanish before the beams of thy brightness. Fill us with holy love, and open to us the treasures of thy wisdom. All our desire is known unto thee; therefore, perfect what thou hast begun, and what thy spirit has awakened in us to ask in prayer. We seek thy face; turn thy face unto us and show us thy glory. Then shall our longings be satisfied, and our peace shall be perfect. Amen.[1]

RESPONSIVE READING:

Leader: Thus saith the high and lofty One that inhabited eternity, whose name is holy.

Group: I dwell in the high and holy place, with him also that is of a contrite and humble spirit, to revive the spirit of the humble, and to revive the heart of the contrite ones.

Leader: Beloved, now are we sons of God, and it doth not yet appear what we shall be: but we know that, when he shall appear, we shall be like him; for we shall see him as he is.

Group: And every man that hath this hope in him purifieth himself, even as he is pure.

Leader: For now we see through a glass darkly, but then face to face.

Group: Now I know in part; but then shall I know even as also I am known.

Leader: Speak to Him thou for he hears, and Spirit with Spirit can meet—

Closer is He than breathing, and nearer than hands and feet.[2]

HYMN:

> Ye fair green hills of Galilee
>   That girdle quiet Nazareth,
> What glorious vision did ye see,
>   When he who conquered sin and death
> Your flowery slopes and summits trod,
>   And grew in grace with man and God?
>
> "We saw no glory crown his head
>   As childhood ripened into youth;
> No angels on his errands sped;
>   He wrought no sign; but meekness, truth,
> And duty marked each step he trod,
>   And love to man, and love to God."
>
> Jesus! my Saviour, Master, King,
>   Who didst for me the burden bear;
> While saints in heaven thy glory sing,
>   Let me on earth thy likeness wear;
> Mine be the path thy feet have trod:
>   Duty, and love to man and God.
>   —EUSTACE R. CONDER

INTERPRETATION OF THE PAINTING:

We treasure the conceptions of Christ which have been given to us by the great artists throughout the ages. We see him pictured in various types according to the nationality of the artist. These

ictures, however, are the product of the imagination of the artist, for
Christ's earthly form has not been passed on to us in statue, or on
anvas. Yet it is amazing that with hundreds of such pictures, no
rtist ever has to place the name on the drawing, for everyone senses
nmediately that it is the Christ.

> No pictured likeness of my Lord have I;
> He carved no record of his ministry
>   On wood or stone.
> He left no sculptured tomb nor parchment dim,
> But trusted for all memory of him
>   Men's hearts alone.[3]

Colonel Henry Stanley Todd, the artist who painted "The Naza-
ene," is an outstanding American, a gentleman of the old school. Hav-
ig painted many masters among men, he had for a long time desired
) paint Christ, the Master of all men. In preparation for the task he
ead and re-read the New Testament, and called into play all his knowl-
dge of men. One afternoon as he was walking in his garden, looking
t the white clouds, the picture of Christ began to form in his mind.
.s it continued to grow clearer, it became so plain that it seemed as
hough he were looking at a real person. At last he had the convic-
ion that the day had come when he must paint the picture of his
esire.

He retired to his room but could not sleep. In the middle of the
ight he went to his studio and stretched a canvas. Then he knelt in
rayer to thank God for the vision which had been given to him.
Carly the next morning he began to paint and continued without in-
erruption until the picture was finished. Within a single day, in
even hours' time, without preliminary drawing, the picture that had
een forming in his mind was transferred to canvas.

The painting at once struck a responsive chord in the hearts of
housands of followers of the Nazarene. It was on exhibition in the
Newhouse Galleries and was shown in the leading churches of New
'ork City and in the larger cities of America. Finally, it was sent
) the World's Fair, in Chicago, where hundreds of thousands viewed
.. So great has been the interest in it that Colonel Todd has allowed
t to be used by The Missionary Education Movement to further the
ause of missions.

Let us notice the difference between this and the conventional pictures of Christ. In this picture the artist has attempted to emphasize the humanity of Christ. Some are startled at first at seeing him with straight features, blue eyes, blond hair, and light complexion. Is there a scriptural basis for depicting the humanity of Christ? The writers of the Gospels spoke of him as being weary, tired, and hungry, and recounted instances when he experienced sorrow and indignation. He came from the carpenter shop, spoke to the people in simple language, and held them by the magnetism of his personality. He attracted people by his broad humanity, his sympathy and understanding. The name he preferred to use in speaking of himself was the "Son of Man." In emphasizing the humanity of Christ the artist is conveying the idea that we today have the same privilege of companionship with Christ, through prayer, as did the disciples and others who knew him in the days of his flesh.

We are accustomed to the sad type, the Man of sorrows, painted by the Italian and Spanish artists. But Colonel Todd has given us a different type. He has shown Jesus as he might have appeared during the Sermon on the Mount, with the listeners just out of sight. Here is the Triumphant Christ who was to be crucified, but would rise again; he who drove the money changers out of the Temple, who faced Pilate and the angry mob, who confounded the accusers of the woman taken in sin. We are the disciples of such a Christ—a Christ who has overcome the world.[4]

> Who sees the face but sees in part; who reads
> The spirit which it hides, sees all, he needs
> No more. Thy grace—
> Thy life in my life, Lord, give thou to me:
> And then, in truth, I may forever see
> My Master's face! [3]

POEM:

> How beauteous were the marks divine,
> That in thy meekness used to shine,
> That lit thy lonely pathway, trod
> In wondrous love, O Son of God!

THE NAZARENE

O wondrous Lord, my soul would be
Still more and more conformed to thee,
And learn of thee, the lowly One,
And like thee, all my journey run.
                    —A. CLEVELAND COXE

LITANY OF SUPPLICATION:

Leader: Thou who taught the thronging people
                    By blue Galilee;
                Speak to us, thy erring children,
                    Teach us purity.

Group: O Lord, reveal thyself to us as we wait in thy presence.

Leader: Thou whose touch could heal the leper,
                    Make the blind to see;
                Touch our hearts and turn the sinning
                    Into purity.

Group: O Lord, forgive our sins and make us pure indeed.

Leader: Thou whose word could still the tempest,
                    Calm the raging sea;
                Hush the storm of human passions,
                    Give us purity.

Group: O Lord, speak to us and give us thy peace.

Leader: Thou who sinless met the tempter;
                    Grant, O Christ, that we
                May o'ercome the bent to evil
                    By thy purity.[5]

Group: O Lord, may a sense of thy presence give to us the power to
    resist evil. AMEN.

HYMN: "O Young and Fearless Prophet," or
    "More Like the Master."

BENEDICTION:

Father, give thy benediction, and may thy presence continue
with us in all the days that are ahead." AMEN.

— 23 —

SERVICE 2

CHRIST WITH MARY AND MARTHA
(*Hendrik Siemiradski*)

AIM: Through meditating upon the message of the painting to lead to greater wisdom in making choices.

PRELUDE: Hymn tune "Diademata."

CALL TO WORSHIP:

> From homes of quiet peace
>   We lift up hands of prayer,
> And those thou gavest us to love
>   Commend, Lord, to thy care.
>
> Let thine almighty arm
>   Be their defense and shield;
> And whosesoever cause is thine
>   To them the victory yield.
> —WILLIAM HENRY DRAPER

HYMN: "O Christ, the Way, the Truth, the Life," or "Jesus Calls Us."

RESPONSIVE READING:

Leader: Now it came to pass, as they went, that he entered into a certain village: and a certain woman, named Martha, received him into her house.

Group: And she had a sister called Mary, which also sat at Jesus' feet, and heard his word.

CHRIST WITH MARY AND MARTHA

Leader: But Martha was cumbered about much serving, and came to him, and said, Lord, dost thou not care that my sister hath left me to serve alone? bid her therefore that she help me.

Group: And Jesus answered and said unto her, Martha, Martha, thou art careful and troubled about many things: but one thing is needful: and Mary hath chosen that good part, which shall not be taken away from her.[1]

PRAYER HYMN:

> Jesus, kneel beside me
>   In the dawn of the day,
> Thine is prayer eternal—
>   Teach me how to pray!
>
> Master, work beside me
>   In the shining sun;
> Gently guide thy servant
>   Till the work be done.
>
> Saviour, watch beside me
>   In the closing light;
> Lo, the evening cometh—
>   Watch with me this night!
>
> Birds are winging homeward,
>   Sun and shadow cease;
> Saviour, take my spirit
>   To thy perfect peace. AMEN.[2]
>   —ALLEN EASTMAN CROSS

POEM:

> O happy home, where thou art loved the dearest,
>   Thou loving Friend, and Saviour of our race,
> And where among the guests there never cometh
>   One who can hold such high and honored place!
>
> O happy home, where each one serves thee, lowly,
>   Whatever his appointed work may be,
> Till every common task seems great and holy,
>   When it is done, O Lord, as unto thee!

— 25 —

PAINTINGS

O happy home, where thou art not forgotten,
　　Where joy is overflowing, full, and free,
O happy home, where every wounded spirit
　　Is brought, Physician, Comforter, to thee.
　　　　　　　　　　　　　—Carl J. P. Spitta

Story of the Painting:

This scene is laid in Palestine. The old olive trees, with the
twisted hollow trunks, are similar to those that grow on Olive
Through the spaces one can see the hills of Judea, and the one-storie
houses of stone in the village. It is all in the picture, even to the hedg
of prickly pear behind the head of Christ. The artist had seen all o
this no doubt on a visit to the Holy Land.

From the account given in the Scripture the artist has inferre
that the home of Mary and Martha is a home of wealth. He ha
painted the wide-spreading villa of white stone; the leisurely approac
with its pergola of vines and its seats for rest; the garden wall t
shade the table by the door; the mullioned window, small and ric
suggesting a noonday refuge from the heat in the spacious hall. N
wonder Jesus loved it.

In this home in Bethany personal service reached a climax; ho
pitality became a fine art. And always behind such hospitality ther
is forethought, anxiety, and perhaps drudgery. There are those wh
prepared the meals and made the rooms comfortable. These person
are indispensable, and yet they receive scant recognition. While the
are bending over the hot stoves in the kitchen, they are missing th
words of wisdom that fall from the mouth of the guest in the living
room.

Martha has come with her pot to draw water. She may have ha
enough already, but she is disturbed that her sister has left her t
serve alone, and this was a good way to call attention to the dutie
still undone. No doubt she clanked the chain for all she could and
rattled the copper pail and perhaps spilled a little water on the cur
so that she might utter an exclamation! But it was all of no use; th
pretty turban beyond the seat never stirred; the ears were deaf. Mary
sitting at the feet of Jesus, was entranced by his conversation.

And now Martha stands irresolute, poising her jar upon the step
and fidgeting with her dress, trying to decide whether to say nothing
and go back to her work, or to give her lazy sister a piece of her mind

he appeals to the Master, "Lord, dost thou not care that my sister
ath left me to serve alone? bid her therefore that she help me."
Sut he replies, "Ah, Martha, Martha, thou art anxious and troubled
bout many things. Thy guest would be pleased with nothing but
igs if he could only see thee here also, feasting thy soul upon his
read, listening to the truths which he is uttering. But one thing is
needful: and Mary hath chosen that good part, which shall not be
taken away from her."

Did Mary know that the Master was coming, and did she bring
her harp out here by the rosebush in the hope of waylaying his tired
feet? How did she await his approach and greeting? Let us not
deceive ourselves. This girl has lost her heart to the noblest of the
sons of men. To look into his face, to hear his words, to sit at his feet,
is to touch all the bounds of bliss. And Jesus knows this also; and he
deals with her so tenderly that almost without pain he transfers her
love to something other than himself—to the poor whom her wealth
can help, to the suffering whom her sympathy can strengthen, and to
all those little ones in loving whom she will still love him. Thus he
gently disengages himself until she begins to see what he has done and
why he did it. His gracious personality merges with the truth which
he teaches until all good seems easy and any sacrifice possible for
his sake.[3]

Poem:

> What is the work that I ought to do,
> Now that the busy day dawns anew?
> For tasks are so many and hours so few!
> Do the work you will long to have done,
> Fight the battle you will wish you had won
> When shadows fall at the last set of sun.
>
> What words should I utter, what message teach,
> Now when human thought and human speech
> Are restless as waves that break on the beach?
> Speak with clear voice, exultant or dread,
> Say the words you will wish you had said
> When the sounding hours have to silence sped.
>
> Life offers such rich gifts manifold—
> Pleasure and honor and love and gold.

Which should I choose to have and to hold?
Out of those treasures so varied and vast
Choose what you'll wish you had chosen at last,
When life with all of its chances is past.[4]

             —EFFIE SMITH ELY

PRAYER:

Our Father, be very near each one of us and grant that we ma
enter into communion with thee. Help us to realize that withou
thee we can do nothing. May our feeling of inadequacy drive us t
depend more and more upon the power which comes from thee. A
far as we are able we offer to thee our entire personality for wha
ever this day may hold. Wilt thou direct our energies and sanctif
to thy purpose all our gifts of mind and intellect? As workers to
gether with thee, grant unto us a greater desire to serve. If we hav
been indifferent to the needs of others, forgive us; if we have bee
too busy to render service to thee, forgive us. Grant unto us a greate
loyalty to thy eternal truths and a great devotion to thee. In Jesu
Name. AMEN.

HYMN: "Sun of My Soul," or

      "A Charge to Keep I Have."

BENEDICTION:

Grant that in the days that are ahead we may serve others a
thou didst serve, and love others as thou dost love. AMEN.

SERVICE 3

THE FRIEND OF THE HUMBLE

(*Leon Augustin L'hermitte*)

AIM: To lead to the conception that the poor are just as much in the thought of God as are the favored.

PRELUDE: "Nocturne in F" by R. Schumann (Opus 23, No. 4).

CALL TO WORSHIP:

> Come, sound his praise abroad,
>   And hymns of glory sing:
> Jehovah is the sovereign God,
>   The universal King.
>
> Come, worship at his throne;
>   Come, bow before the Lord:
> We are his works, and not our own;
>   He formed us by his word.
>
> Today attend his voice,
>   Nor dare provoke his rod;
> Come, like the people of his choice,
>   And own your gracious God.
> —ISAAC WATTS

HYMN: "Jesus, the Very Thought of Thee," or "O Young and Fearless Prophet."

RESPONSIVE READING:
Leader: Blessed are the poor in spirit: for theirs is the kingdom of heaven.

Group: Blessed are they that mourn: for they shall be comforted.

Leader: Blessed are the meek: for they shall inherit the earth.

Group: Blessed are they which do hunger and thirst after righteousness: for they shall be filled.

Leader: Trust in the Lord, and do good: so shalt thou dwell in the land, and verily thou shalt be fed.

Group: Delight thyself also in the Lord; and he shall give thee the desires of thine heart.

Leader: Commit thy way unto the Lord; trust also in him, and he shall bring it to pass.

Group: The steps of a good man are ordered by the Lord; and he delighteth in his way. Though he fall, he shall not be utterly cast down: for the Lord upholdeth him with his hand.

Leader: I have been young, and now am old; yet have I not seen the righteous forsaken, nor his seed begging bread.

Group: Mark the perfect man, and behold the upright: for the end of that man is peace.[1]

Prayer:

O God, thou who hast prepared for those who love thee such good things as pass man's understanding: Pour into our hearts such love toward thee, that we, loving thee above all things, may obtain thy promises, which exceed all that we can desire; through Jesus Christ our Lord. Amen.[2]

Poem:

> Our Master toiled, a carpenter
>   Of busy Galilee;
> He knew the weight of ardent tasks;
>   Ofttimes, wearily,
> He sought, apart, in earnest prayer
> For strength, beneath his load of care.
>
> He took a manly share of work,
>   No thoughtless shirker he.
> From dawn to dusk, before his bench,
>   He labored faithfully.

THE FRIEND OF THE HUMBLE

He felt just pride in work well done
And found rest sweet, at setting sun.

His Father worked, and he rejoiced
  That honest toil was his—
To whom was given grace to know
  Divinest mysteries:
And shall not we find toiling good
Who serve in labor's brotherhood? [3]

—THOMAS CURTIS CLARK

OFFERTORY.

OFFERING RESPONSE:

Saviour, thy dying love
  Thou gavest me,
Nor should I aught withhold,
  Dear Lord, from thee;
In love my soul would bow,
My heart fulfill its vow,
Some offering bring thee now,
  Something for thee. AMEN.

—SYLVANUS D. PHELPS

INTERPRETATION OF THE PAINTING:

When we look at this canvas with its cool tones of quiet color, we need no interpreter to tell the artist's meaning or to give a title to the picture. There comes rushing to our minds a scene on the first Easter Day.

As the sun hangs low over the western hills we see three weary travelers enter the town of Emmaus and pause before a door. One of the men, with a word of farewell, turns down the street, but he is detained by the urgency of his companions, who insist on his remaining with them. The three enter and sit down at supper. The guest takes a loaf of bread, and, breaking it, looks upward in thanksgiving. Astonishment is written on the faces of the other men, for they recognize the countenance of their Master, dead yesterday, but alive today.

The artist has so portrayed him, in each hand a piece of the broken loaf, his eyes uplifted in communion with his Father. This much is clear, but what is the meaning of the chairs, the table and the men in European costume? Their appearance is unquestionably that of French workingmen. The surroundings are those of a humble French home. What does it mean? The artist was not ignorant of historic accuracy, but he has a definite purpose in mind. He is trying to impress us with the thought that what occurred to those Hebrews on their journey and in the humble home may happen every day in any country.

By taking a biblical incident and placing it in a present-day setting and choosing his characters from the humble French peasants, the artist is saying that Jesus is striving to make himself known today in the workingman's home. He is portraying the fact that the people who live simply and plainly are just as much in Jesus' thought as are the most wealthy and favored in all the land. Jesus went into the homes of the poor, took things as they were, and made the home radiant with his presence. He won the hearts of the poor, for, having toiled for his daily bread, he knew their problems. He did not have one gospel for the cultured and another for the illiterate. There is not one saying of his that need have been obscure to the unlearned, for he spoke in a language which all understood.

The artist is portraying this thought that Jesus is unseen but his presence is about us at all times. We walk amid the unseen, but Jesus would, at any time, cease to be unseen if only our eyes were opened and we lived as though we were in his presence. The disciples, as they walked to Emmaus, were talking of Jesus, and he came to them. As Jesus graced the homes of the first century by his presence, so may the humblest home today be blest by a sense of his presence. The companionship of the Master is within the reach of every one of us every day, if we would become aware of his presence and live as though we were seeing him who is invisible.[4]

POEM:

> If I should ask, of him who holds
> All good within his giving,
> Some special boon, I think I'd ask
> For grace in living.
>
> That I may find some clear delight
> In small, sweet gifts of beauty;
> Nor miss the harmony divine
> In simplest duty.

CHRIST WITH MARY AND MARTHA, by Hendrik Siemiradski

THE FRIEND OF THE HUMBLE, by Leon Augustin L'hermitte

DEATH THE VICTOR, by Robert Lindneux

THE FRIEND OF THE HUMBLE

That toil may catch the radiance
   Of love's imprismed color;
And sacrifice be joy that dares
   To make life fuller.

That I may have a gentle heart,
   A spirit brave and gay,
A comrade's sympathy for those
   Who walk my way;

The proud humility that's blest
   Receiving as in giving—
Lord, teach me daily, then, the art
   Of gracious living! [5]

            —EDITH KENT BATTLE

PRAYER:

Almighty and everlasting God, who art more ready to hear than we to pray, and who art wont to give more than either we desire or deserve; pour down upon us the abundance of thy mercy, forgiving us those things whereof our conscience is afraid and giving us those good things which we are not worthy to ask, except through the merits and mediation of Jesus Christ thy Son. Grant us in our doubts and uncertainties the grace to ask what thou wouldst have us to do, that the Spirit of Wisdom may save us from false choices, and that in thy light we may see light, and in thy straight path may not stumble.[6] Grant us an awareness of thy presence, help us to walk as though we were in thy presence at all times, and whatever our appointed work may be, grant that every common task seem great, because we are doing it as unto thee. In Jesus' name. AMEN.

HYMN: "O Master Workman of the Race," or
      "Lord, for Tomorrow and Its Needs."

BENEDICTION:

May the peace of God rule in your hearts and abide with you evermore. AMEN.

SERVICE 4

DEATH THE VICTOR
(*Robert Lindneux*)

AIM: To lead to a new realization of the horror and futility of war and to a desire to further our peace-loving position.

PRELUDE: Hymn tune "National Hymn."

CALL TO WORSHIP:

> God of our fathers, whose almighty hand
> Leads forth in beauty all the starry band
> Of shining worlds in splendor through the skies,
> Our grateful songs before thy throne arise.
>
> Thy love divine hath led us in the past,
> In this free land by thee our lot is cast;
> Be thou our ruler, guardian, guide, and stay,
> Thy word our law, thy paths our chosen way.
>
> From war's alarms, from deadly pestilence,
> Be thy strong arm our ever sure defense;
> Thy true religion in our hearts increase,
> Thy bounteous goodness nourish us in peace.
> —DANIEL C. ROBERTS

HYMN: "God of the Nations, Near and Far," or
"These Things Shall Be."

UNISON SCRIPTURE READING:
Blessed are the peacemakers: for they shall be called the children of God.

DEATH THE VICTOR

Love your enemies, bless them that curse you, do good to them that hate you, and pray for them which despitefully use you and persecute you.

All things whatsoever ye would that men should do to you, do ye even so to them.

But I say unto you, that ye resist not evil.

Recompense to no man evil for evil.

If thine enemy hunger, feed him; if he thirst, give him drink.

Be not overcome of evil, but overcome evil with good.[1]

PRAYER:

In the name of those who died
On the fields blood-drenched and wide,
Who gave up joyous life
In a war to end all strife,
Father, this Armistice Day,
For peace on earth we pray.

We cry to thee for the sake
Of hearts which now quiver and break,
Of bodies tortured, destroyed,
Of homes that are ruined and void:
Father, this Armistice Day
For peace on earth we pray.

For love of the children who wait
The future, untroubled by hate,
Upon whose innocent years
No shadow of doom yet appears,
Father, this Armistice Day,
Give peace on earth, we pray. AMEN.[2]
— EFFIE SMITH ELY

HYMN: "At Length There Dawns the Glorious Day."

SCRIPTURE:

They shall beat their swords into plowshares, and their spears into pruninghooks: nation shall not lift up sword against nation, neither shall they learn war any more.[3]

PAINTINGS

Robert Lindneux, the artist who painted "Death the Victor," is c Swiss-French ancestry. At an early age he began to express himse. in colors and at sixteen went abroad to study in Paris, Berlin, Municl and Dusseldorf. Returning to the United States after a long absence he established his residence in the West, where he has lived in cov camps, on stock ranches, and with miners in lonely cabins far remove from centers of civilization. He was adopted by a tribe of Sioux Ir dians, who taught him their customs, traditions, and legends. Thu by gaining first-hand knowledge of their ways of living he was abl to transfer some of their customs to canvas.

Many of the art critics have commented favorably on Mr. Linc neux's paintings. When one of his pictures was on exhibition is Chicago, Mr. C. J. Bulliet, the art critic, said, "Mr. Lindneux is n stranger to Chicago. He has exhibited in former years in the gallerie of Marshall Field. One of his well-remembered paintings is of horse looking out of the upper half of a barn door—the lower hal closed and latched. It was necessary to keep a guard on watch les visitors soil the painting by trying to unlatch the very realistic latcl and let the horse out. And on the mountain out of Denver, wher Buffalo Bill's body is buried, there is in his memorial cabin a paintin by Lindneux so realistic that the Indians pay homage to it, declarin that the spirit of the scout is enchained and lives in the portrait." [4]

Mr. Lindneux's painting "Death the Victor" created a sensatior when it was exhibited at the Findlay galleries in Chicago, where it wa seen by thousands of people. The artist has exerted himself to th utmost in producing this huge allegorical picture, the purpose o which is to portray the horror and futility of war. Every once in while the world feels that it has outgrown this primitive form of ex pression, allegory; but the most sophisticated often revert to it when they wish to portray an idea with all of its stark realism.

In this picture the grim fleshless image of Death in full regimen tal regalia of a commanding officer is mounted on a horse, a magnifi cent animal. With drawn sword held aloft, dripping with the bloo of slaughtered youth of the world, Death rides over the fallen sol diers of all wars from the World War back to the Trojans and re ceding far into the mists before the dawn of history.

Accustomed as we are to thinking of death in connection witl shrouds and mausoleums, we are at first startled at seeing him arraye in a uniform of dazzling colors, with all the pomp of world conquerors from Alexander to Napoleon. Upon closer examination his armor will be found to be made up of fragments of many uniforms that have made warriors seem magnificent. He is wearing a gold helmet on his skull and he stares at the beholder through sightless sockets.

As we study the picture we discover that the artist is meticulously accurate. The uniform of each fallen soldier in the foreground is correct in every detail, enabling us to pick out the youth of France, England, the United States, Italy, Germany and Austria, all huddled together, covering the battlefield. In the distance are the ruins of ancient buildings, typifying the civilizations of different periods in the world's history; and rising out of the background are the black clouds which form a canopy over it all. One looks among the dead for those who make wars, but in vain. Youth and youth only is what one sees, strewn about in blood-stiffened uniforms like chaff, while Death rides ruthlessly on to newer conquests.

In the opinion of many critics Mr. Lindneux has produced a great painting. If a sufficient number of people absorb its message, it will go a long way toward establishing world peace. The artist has stated very definitely his stand against war, and he is trying to impress us with the truth that regardless of which army is victorious the ultimate victor is always death. In his passion for universal peace Mr. Lindneux does not go as a soldier bearing arms; but in his studio, with pigments and canvas, he is making his contribution to humanity by creating a sentiment against war.

When the artist was asked for his idea back of the picture he replied: "My inspiration for the picture is centered around the fact that it has always been a source of deep regret to me that in our civilized day nations do not seem to be able to settle their differences by arbitration. Instead they resort to war, where the ultimate victor is always death, besides leaving a trail of untold suffering and hardship in its wake for many years thereafter."

POEM:

> Peace in our time, O Lord,
> To all the peoples—Peace!
> Peace surely based upon thy will
> And built in righteousness.

Thy power alone can break
The fetters that enchain
The sorely-stricken soul of life,
And make it live again.

Too long mistrust and fear
Have held our souls in thrall;
Sweep through the earth, keen breath of heaven,
And sound a nobler call!
    Come, as thou didst of old,
    In love so great that men
    Shall cast aside all other gods
    And turn to thee again!

O shall we never learn
The truth all time has taught—
That without God as architect
Our building comes to naught?
    Lord, help us, and inspire
    Our hearts and lives, that we
    May build, with all thy wondrous gifts,
    A Kingdom meet for thee!

Peace in our time, O Lord,
To all the peoples—Peace!
Peace that shall build a glad new world,
And make for life's increase.
    O Living Christ, who still
    Dost all our burdens share,
    Come now and dwell within the hearts
    Of all men everywhere! [5]

—JOHN OXENHAM

LITANY OF SUPPLICATION:

Leader: God of all nations, we pray for all the people of the earth.

Group: Hear our prayer, we beseech thee.

Leader: Deliver us from the evils which obstruct the coming of thy
    kingdom in the world.

Group: Hear our prayer, we beseech thee.

Leader: Help us to uproot all selfishness, prejudice, hatred, or ill will which is found in our hearts.

Group: Hear our prayer, we beseech thee.

Leader: Forgive us for our distrust of other nations.

Group: Hear our prayer, we beseech thee.

Leader: Forgive us for putting our trust in weapons of war.

Group: Hear our prayer, we beseech thee.

Leader: Give us greater faith in love, and help us to place our dependence in good will.

Group: Hear our prayer, we beseech thee.

Leader: Help us to live together in peace as children of a common Father.

Group: Hear our prayer, we beseech thee.

Leader: Reveal thy purpose to us.

Group: In Jesus' name. AMEN.

HYMN: "Lead On, O King Eternal."

BENEDICTION:

> May the peace of Christ our Saviour,
> The Father's boundless love,
> With the Holy Spirit's favor,
> Rest upon us from above. AMEN.

SERVICE 5

CHRIST IN GETHSEMANE

(*Heinrich Hofmann*)

AIM: To help the group to realize that it is only through supreme endeavor that one produces real achievements.

PRELUDE: Hymn tune "Ton-Y-Botel."

CALL TO WORSHIP:

The hour cometh, and now is, when the true worshipers shall worship the Father in spirit and in truth: for the Father seeketh such to worship him. God is a Spirit: and they that worship him must worship him in spirit and in truth.

HYMN: "When I Survey the Wondrous Cross," or
       "Above the Hills of Time the Cross Is Gleaming."

RESPONSIVE READING:

Leader: Who hath believed our report? and to whom hath the arm of the Lord been revealed?

Group: For he grew up before him as a tender plant, and as a root out of a dry ground;

Leader: He was despised, and rejected of men; a man of sorrows, and acquainted with grief:

Group: And we hid as it were our faces from him; he was despised and we esteemed him not.

Leader: Surely he hath borne our griefs, and carried our sorrows:

Group: Yet we did esteem him stricken, smitten of God, and afflicted

CHRIST IN GETHSEMANE

Leader: But he was wounded for our transgressions; he was bruised for our iniquities:

Group: The chastisement of our peace was upon him: and with his stripes we are healed.

Leader: And the Lord hath laid on him the iniquity of us all.

Group: He was oppressed, yet when he was afflicted he opened not his mouth;

Leader: As a lamb that is led to the slaughter, and as a sheep that before its shearers is dumb, so he opened not his mouth.

Group: He poured out his soul unto death, and was numbered with the transgressors; and he bare the sins of many.[1]

HYMN: " 'Tis Midnight, and on Olive's Brow," or "Must Jesus Bear the Cross Alone?"

POEM:

> More things are wrought by prayer
> Than this world dreams of. Wherefore let thy voice
> Rise like a fountain for me night and day.
> For what are men better than sheep or goats
> That nourish a blind life within the brain,
> If, knowing God, they lift not hands in prayer
> Both for themselves and those who call them friends?
> For so the whole round earth is every way
> Bound by gold chains about the feet of God.
> —ALFRED TENNYSON

POEM:

> I asked for bread; God gave a stone instead.
> Yet, while I pillowed there my weary head,
> The angels made a ladder of my dreams,
> Which upward to celestial mountains led.
> And when I woke beneath the morning's beams,
> Around my resting-place fresh manna lay;
> And, praising God, I went upon my way.
> For I was fed.

PAINTINGS

God answers prayer, sometimes, when hearts are weak,
He gives the very gifts believers seek.
But often faith must learn a deeper rest,
And trust God's silence when he does not speak;
For he whose name is Love will send the best.
Stars may burn out, nor mountain walls endure,
But God is true, his promises are sure
  For those who seek.

—AUTHOR UNKNOWN

SCRIPTURE:

And he went a little farther, and fell on his face, and prayed, saying, O my Father, if it be possible, let this cup pass from me! nevertheless, not as I will, but as thou wilt.[2]

INTERPRETATION OF THE PAINTING:

Before such a scene we are silent—the soul is hushed in the presence of this cry of suffering. A mystery broods over this midnight scene in the Master's life. Let us withdraw into the shadows and consider its meaning. Let us meditate, not upon its message of sorrowing, but on its call to heroic service. Back of every supreme achievement is supreme endeavor. Great achievements are wrought by those who have the capacity, the patience, and the courage to go a little further than anyone else has yet ventured.

In this picture Jesus goes a little further in the accomplishment of the world's supreme achievement—the expression of God's personality in human character. Just as the toilers who have it in their hearts to render a surpassing service find themselves gradually separated from the multitude, so Jesus went a little further, went into the night beyond human help and pity, to endure the loneliness of the hero and the thinker. The acceptance of loneliness is the necessary condition to all rare achievement.[3]

The chief point in this picture is the emphasis it lays on the loneliness of Jesus. The first law of heroism is the courage to go on when others are left behind. The artist has wisely given to his hero a regal aspect, that of an uncrowned king, for so he was. The light about his head is the artist's way of saying what Luke says, that an angel from heaven strengthened him. It was his filial trust and his knowledge of his Father's approval, which never deserted him through it all

CHRIST IN GETHSEMANE

With his Father's approval of his heroic struggle, he came out from the olive grove "well content with death and shame," and walked henceforth through his remaining passion with the mien of a conqueror.

The sight of the solitary sufferer in Gethsemane has been and will continue to be, so long as art remains, one of the mightiest redemptive forces in human life. It made sin seem a new thing. The sin that caused such suffering could not henceforth be looked upon lightly. Gethsemane is the best corrective of the theory that sin is only "involuntary error." Men become conscious of sin, as never before, when they look at it through the eyes of Christ. Such a sight supplies the strongest motive to keep men from sin, and it will operate when all others have failed.

Gethsemane is a challenge to all men to be heroic. The trial question it puts to every man is whether he will follow Jesus in his Gethsemane. "You cannot," says Ruskin, "save men from death but by facing it for them; nor from sin but by resisting it for them. That is the final doctrine, the inevitable one, not of Christianity only, but of all heroic faith; and the first trial question of a true soul to itself must always be—'Have I a religion, have I a country, have I a love that I am ready to die for?' This is the root of heroism. Only those who grasp it can be heroes."

Jesus left eight of his disciples at the outer gate of the olive garden. A little later he parted from Peter, James, and John also and was left alone. Can it be that no one was able to watch with him in his lonely struggle? Who can follow in his train? [4]

POEM:

> Under an Eastern sky
> Amid a rabble cry,
> A man went forth to die
>   For me!
>
> Thorn-crowned his blessed head,
> Blood-stained his every tread,
> Cross-laden on he sped,
>   For me!
>
> Pierced through his hands and feet,
> Three hours o'er him did beat,

Fierce rays of noontide heat,
 For me!

Thus wert thou made all mine;
Lord, make me wholly thine,
Give grace and strength divine
 To me!

In thought and word and deed,
Thy will to do; oh! lead my feet,
E'en though they bleed,
 To thee!
     —AUTHOR UNKNOWN

HYMN: "Into the Woods My Master Went," or
   "In the Hour of Trial."

PRAYER:

O thou Divine Companion, we thank thee for the strength which comes from communion with thee. We are grateful that in times of moral crisis we can come to thee for guidance. As we think of Christ's seeking strength through fellowship with thee, we would look to thee for direction in daily living. May we have thy spirit with us leading us in the direction of the right. Grant unto us the strength to go against the crowd, to be unpopular, if need be, in order to maintain our ideals. Give us the courage to stand steadfastly for the right and to live according to the best we know. Forgive us if we have ever compromised our principles for the sake of the pleasure of the moment. Give us a new vision of our own powers and possibilities and deepen the desire to attain them. For Jesus' sake. AMEN.

BENEDICTION:

Let the words of my mouth and the meditation of my heart be acceptable in thy sight, O Lord, my Strength and my Redeemer. AMEN.

SERVICE 6

FOR HE HAD GREAT POSSESSIONS
(*George Frederick Watts*)

AIM: To lead to a new conception of the Christian attitude toward material possessions.

PRELUDE: Hymn tune "Corwin."

CALL TO WORSHIP:

O come let us worship and bow down, let us kneel before the Lord our Maker.

God is light and in him is no darkness at all.

O Lord, send out thy light and thy truth, let them lead us to thy holy hill.

God is love, and he that dwelleth in love dwelleth in God.

Shed thy love abroad in our hearts, and keep us ever in thy love.

HYMN: "Awake, Awake to Love and Work," or
"God's Trumpet Wakes the Slumbering World."

SCRIPTURE:

And behold, one came, and said unto him, Good Master, what good thing shall I do, that I may have eternal life? And he said unto him, Why callest thou me good? there is none good but one, that is, God; but if thou wilt enter into life, keep the commandments. He saith unto him, Which? Jesus said, Thou shalt do no murder, Thou shalt not commit adultery, Thou shalt not steal, Thou shalt not bear false witness, Honour thy father and thy mother; and, Thou shalt love thy neighbour as thyself. The young man saith unto him, All these things have I kept from my youth up: what lack I yet? Jesus said

unto him, If thou wilt be perfect, go and sell that thou hast, and give
to the poor, and thou shalt have treasure in heaven; and come and
follow me. But when the young man heard that saying, he went
away sorrowful: for he had great possessions.[1]

LITANY OF THANKS:

Leader: Our Father in heaven, from whom cometh every good and
perfect gift,

Group: We thank thee for all thy goodness.

Leader: For thy Spirit which makes us conscious of our need of thee

Group: We give thee thanks.

Leader: For a vision of our own powers and capabilities

Group: We give thee thanks.

Leader: For the glow of health, the capacity to labor, and the privilege
of serving others

Group: We give thee thanks.

Leader: For a proper sense of values, a Christian attitude toward
money and other possessions

Group: We give thee thanks.

Leader: Help us to choose the best at all times and put aside those
things that are base and ignoble.

Group: For Jesus' sake. AMEN.

POEM:

> Thy spirit be upon us, Lord,
>   Thy truth illumine our way,
> Thy love unfathomed fill each soul,
>   Thy courage be our stay.
>
> Thyself be our companion, Lord,
>   Thy mind be in our mind,
> Thy heart be in our wayward heart
>   Till life and peace we find.

FOR HE HAD GREAT POSSESSIONS

Thyself be in our life, O Lord,
Thy beauty and good will,
Thy serving grace our meat and drink,
Till thy life we fulfill.[2]
—CHAUNCEY R. PIETY

HYMN: "In Life's Earnest Morning."

STORY OF THE ARTIST AND THE PAINTING:

George Frederick Watts, the poet-painter of England, was the son of a piano tuner. He began to draw while still a lad, and by the time he was twelve years old was a prolific illustrator. At the age of twenty he attracted considerable notice by winning a prize of $1,500 for a decoration for the House of Parliament. He used this money for traveling in Italy that he might study the works of the great masters. Winning another prize of $2,500 gave him an enviable position as an artist.

Watts was attracted to Miss Ellen Terry, the popular English actress, because of her beauty. She became the model for Sir Galahad, one of his most famous pictures. They were married when she was only sixteen years of age, but their marriage resulted in failure and was dissolved in a short while. Later he married Miss Mary Fraser Tytler, and this union brought rare happiness to both of them.

Many honors came to Watts, but he remained modest and humble and held to his purpose of expressing great truths through his art. "My intention," he said, "has not been so much to paint pictures that will charm the eye as to suggest great thoughts that will appeal to the imagination, and kindle all that is best and noblest in humanity. I want to teach people how to live, how to make use of all their powers, to work and hope and enjoy life, not to be mere slaves and drudges, but to care for something higher than money-making and selfish pleasure." His life was marked by singleness of purpose and was wholly devoted to art. The charm of his personality and the simplicity of his life impressed all who knew him, but he never cared for society as the term is popularly understood.

A larger share of public recognition came to Watts than he desired. He did not try to appeal to popular favor. Twice a baronetcy in England was offered to him, but each time he courteously declined. It was only when the Order of Merit was established that he could be induced to accept any mark of public honor from his country. Oxford conferred upon him the degree of Doctor of Civil Law, and Cambridge the degree of Doctor of Laws. France conferred upon him the Cross of the Legion of Honor, and Italy made him a Knight of the Order of San Luigi. After he became a man of wealth, he refused to work for private individuals, and gave generously of his time to his country. Many of his pictures were donated to leading cities in various countries. A replica of his "Love and Life" was sent to America and now hangs in the White House.

Watts did more than any other artist of his time to raise portrait painting to a high degree of excellence. He painted over 150 portraits of well-known men, including Tennyson, Carlyle, Browning, and others. These he donated to England to be hung in the National Portrait Gallery. Ruskin spoke of him as a painter of thought and history, but the artist does not make such claims for himself. He had something to say, and he used his art to express it. He believed that the purpose of art is to urge men to higher thought and action, and certainly his symbolic paintings have kindled in many a desire for nobler living.

Among his scriptural paintings that of the rich young ruler ranks highest. In this three-quarter-length picture the face is entirely hidden; so we must refer to the Scripture for the details. We are told that he is a young man, a ruler, and that he came to Jesus inquiring the way of life. That he is rich we judge by the clothes, the silk turban and sleeve, the velvet and fur of his mantle. From the rings on his fingers and the golden chain about his shoulder we infer that he loved showy adornment.

There is an atmosphere of indefiniteness about the picture until we come to the hand, which is large but not beautiful. The fingers are like talons which will come together with a viselike grip, not to open until he sees some new object of desire. From this we infer that the young man is dominated by his money, that he is swallowed up by his passion to accumulate. All that gives him distinction as a person made in God's image dies out, and only the elemental function of grabbing remains. That is why the artist does not show his face. When the love of money takes possession, one by one the virtues leave and the vices arrive. First the fountains of sympathy are stopped; then arises the will to dominate rather than to serve. Jesus knew the whole tragic result of this way of living; so he commanded the young man, "Go and sell that thou hast, and give to the poor, and thou shalt have treasure in heaven; and come and follow me."

The young man has come to Jesus with the question that has been uppermost in his mind for some time. He realizes that there is something lacking in his life which money cannot supply. Jesus is showing him the greatest thing in the world, but it is too great for him. Jesus knows that his only hope is in giving away all his property. Perhaps the young man says to himself, "I shall have to think about that." As the silent battle goes on, he decides that he cannot face the world without the protection of his riches. With sorrow in his heart, he turns away from Jesus and makes what Dante calls the "great refusal." [3]

We know not what became of him,
  The rich young ruler, high and proud,
Who ran to Jesus in the way
  And knelt before him in the crowd.

"Good Master," murmured he, but when
  Jesus with love and yearning cried,
"Sell all thou hast and follow me!"
  The splendor from his dark eyes died.

As back to ease and power he turned,
  I wonder if a deep unrest
Would nevermore let him forget
  That he had forfeited life's best.

Or did the slowly gathering dust
  Of worldly cares his spirit dim,
Till visions of the perfect way
  No longer lured or troubled him?

Somber, against the centuries
  He stands, who heard the call supreme,
Who loved, but did not own, his Lord,
  Who saw, but followed not, truth's gleam. [4]
                              —Effie Smith Ely

PAINTINGS

As my crowded years sweep on apace,
Am I giving to God the second place?

Hurrying to work, do I fail to pray
And seek his guidance at dawn of day?

Have worldly companions made more dim
My sense of his presence, my love for him?

Have I neglected to do his will,
That my own small plans I might fulfill?

Have I let my cares and worries increase
Till they crowd out from my life his peace?

Pardon me, Father of infinite grace,
If I have given thee second place!

Henceforth be thou first, all others above—
First in my thought and my work and my love.[8]
—Effie Smith Ely

Hymn: "Once to Every Man and Nation," or
"Saviour, Thy Dying Love," or
"Give Me Thy Heart."

Benediction:

Lord, dismiss us with thy blessing and fill our hearts with thy love and peace. Amen.

SIR GALAHAD

(*George Frederick Watts*)

AIM: To lead the group to a new insight of the value of purity of thought, motive, and conduct.

PRELUDE: "The Heavens Are Telling" (Haydn).

CALL TO WORSHIP:

The Lord is in his holy temple: let all the earth keep silence before him.

Surely the Lord is in this place. This is none other than the house of God, and this is the gate of heaven. One thing have I asked of the Lord, that will I seek after; that I may dwell in the house of the Lord all the days of my life, to gaze upon the beauty of the Lord, and to inquire in his temple.

O that I may be filled with the goodness of thy house, the holiness of thy temple.

HYMN: "Purer, Yet Purer," or
"Awake, Awake to Love and Work," or
"True-hearted, Whole-hearted."

RESPONSIVE READING:

Leader: Lord, who shall abide in thy tabernacle? who shall dwell in thy holy hill?

Group: He that walketh uprightly, and worketh righteousness, and speaketh the truth in his heart.

Leader: He that backbiteth not with his tongue, nor doeth evil to his neighbor, nor taketh up a reproach against his neighbor.

PAINTINGS

Group: In whose eyes a vile person is contemned; but he honoreth them that fear the Lord.

Leader: He that sweareth to his own hurt, and changeth not. He that putteth not out his money to usury, nor taketh reward against the innocent.

Group: He that doeth these things shall never be moved.

Leader: Who shall ascend into the hill of the Lord? Who shall stand in his holy place?

Group: He that hath clean hands, and a pure heart; who hath not lifted up his soul unto vanity, and hath not sworn deceitfully.[1]

UNISON PRAYER:

Eternal Father, thou knowest our needs before we even ask. Help us to understand our errors; cleanse us from secret faults; keep us from presumptuous sins; let them not have dominion over us; then shall we be upright, and innocent from the great transgression. Let the words of our mouths and the meditation of our hearts be acceptable in thy sight, O Lord, our strength and our redeemer. AMEN.

POEM:

> Youth, O Youth, can I reach you,
>   Can I speak and make you hear?
> Can I open your eyes to see me?
>   Can my presence draw you near?
>
> Is there a prophet among you,
>   One with a heart to know?
> I will flash my secrets on him,
>   He shall watch my glory grow.
>
> For I, the God, the Father,
>   The Quest, the Final Goal,
> Still search for a prophet among you,
>   To speak my word in his soul.
>   —ANONYMOUS

STORY:

"The quest of the Holy Grail has gripped the imagination of poets and painters alike from early days to our own time. But the supernatural cannot easily be set down in terms of the natural, either in poetry or in painting, a difficulty which both Tennyson and Watts faced with courage and with a degree of success." [2] Tennyson brought the story of the search of the youthful knight within our reach and has made the legend live again in his *Idylls of the King;* Watts has given a vivid portrayal of the moment when the search was rewarded in his picture, "Sir Galahad." Here we see a delicate blending of knightly heroism and religious aspiration. In some of Watts' pictures the idea is so complex that the meaning is difficult to grasp, but in this one the subject speaks for itself. The spirit of the knight is clearly seen in the upstanding figure of the young man.

Many of the knights of King Arthur dedicated themselves to the great purpose of searching for the Holy Grail. This mystic symbol, however, is such that it is veiled from the eyes of all except the pure in heart. Sir Galahad, the youngest of the knights, was the only one able to keep his eyes fixed on the goal until he achieved, but it meant resisting temptation on the one hand and a life of ease on the other. This fearless knight of the pure heart saw the Grail, clear and distinct, while it was veiled from the others by a cloud.

As Sir Galahad rode through the forest the heavenly music of the Grail came to him. Springing from his horse, he stands in an attitude of deep reverence, fascinated with the vision which lights up his face and armor. The woody background, the tangled vegetation, the figure of the knight with his auburn hair and dark armor, and the white horse beside him are familiar objects to us. The artist has portrayed the moment when the knight first caught the glimpse of the Grail by the rapt expression on his face as he gazes at the heavenly vision through a break in the trees. The Grail, however, is not visible to other eyes than those of Sir Galahad. It is left to our imagination.

It is significant that the vision came to the youngest knight but was withheld from the other knights. Visions have always come to the youth, but virtue is not in youthfulness alone. It is in clarity of vision, and in the ardor and enthusiasm with which the youthful strive to make their dreams come true. The artist has given in Sir Galahad, the Pure of Heart, an example of youthful fervor, manly purity, and high idealism. Because of his purity of heart he had a greater insight which enabled him to see visions withheld from others. One of the knights of the Round Table testified to this truth when he said:

"That every evil word I had spoken once,
And every evil thought I had thought of old,
And every evil deed I ever did
Spoke and cried, 'This quest is not for thee.'"

But Sir Galahad, the Pure of Heart, could say to the king:

"I saw the Holy Grail and heard a cry—
O Galahad! and O Galahad, follow me!"

"Ah, Galahad, Galahad," said the king, "for such
As thou art is the vision, not for these."

The artist in picturing the sword hanging by the side of the knight is saying that the young man had not only power of vision, but power of achievement as well. He is illustrating the idea that in goodness there is strength, in evil there is weakness. Sir Galahad voices this truth in these words:

"My strength is as the strength of ten
Because my heart is pure."

Poem:

Let me stand upon the hilltop
Like a tree against the sky.
Let me mark the way for travelers—
Rooted deep, and pointing high.

Here surveyors chart their courses,
Climbers, lost, regain the trail,
Kneel, with new and clearer vision
Of the long-sought Holy Grail.

Keep me pure, O Breath of God,
Worthy of this crest so high!
Help me stand upon the hilltop
Like a tree against the sky.[3]

—J. Lester Hankins

SIR GALAHAD

"To the Knights in the Days of Old," or
"Now in the Days of Youth," or
"O Jesus, Youth of Nazareth."

PRAYER:

O God, thou Searcher of men's hearts, help us to draw near to thee in sincerity and in truth. We thank thee for every good impulse which comes from thee. Reveal unto us the impurities in our lives which keep us from being used of thee. We would consecrate every faculty of mind and body to thy service. Take away from us any indifference or low aim which would keep us from following thee completely. Strengthen and increase our admiration for honest dealing and high living. Help us to live above the common level of life. Strengthen us as we choose the harder right instead of the easier wrong, and may we never be content with a half truth when a whole can be won. May we find genuine pleasure in clean and wholesome fun, and feel a deep disgust for all things low and mean. Inspire us with new visions as we strive to live out thy purpose in the world. In the name of the Master of us all, we pray. AMEN.

BENEDICTION:

Our Father, be our strength and shield and lead us into the way everlasting. AMEN.

THE MAGDALENE

(*Correggio*)

Aim: To lead to a clearer conception of the creative power of love.

Prelude: Hymn tune "Mercy."

Call to Worship:

> Lord, we come before thee now,
> At thy feet we humbly bow;
> O do not our suit disdain;
> Shall we seek thee, Lord, in vain?
>
> Lord, on thee our souls depend;
> In compassion now descend;
> Fill our hearts with thy rich grace,
> Tune our lips to sing thy praise.
>
> In thine own appointed way,
> Now we seek thee, here we stay;
> Lord, we know not how to go,
> Till a blessing thou bestow.
>
> —William Hammond

Hymn: "Immortal Love, Forever Full," or
"Love Divine, All Loves Excelling."

Responsive Reading:

Leader: Have mercy upon me, O God, according to thy lovingkindness; according unto the multitude of thy tender mercies blot out my transgressions.

Group: Wash me thoroughly from mine iniquity, and cleanse me from my sin.

Leader: For I acknowledge my transgressions; and my sin is ever before me.

Group: Against thee, thee only, have I sinned, and done this evil in thy sight; that thou mightest be justified when thou speakest, and be clear when thou judgest.

Leader: Purge me with hyssop, and I shall be clean: wash me, and I shall be whiter than snow.

Group: Create in me a clean heart, O God; and renew a right spirit within me.

Leader: Restore unto me the joy of thy salvation; and uphold me with thy free Spirit.

Group: O Lord, open thou my lips; and my mouth shall show forth thy praise.

Leader: For thou desirest not sacrifice, else would I give it: thou delightest not in burnt offering.

Group: The sacrifices of God are a broken spirit: a broken and a contrite heart, O God, thou wilt not despise.[1]

PRAYER:

Almighty and most merciful Father, we have erred and strayed from thy ways like lost sheep. We have followed the devices and desires of our own hearts. We have offended against thy holy laws. We have left undone those things which we ought to have done; and we have done those things which we ought not to have done. But, thou, O Lord, have mercy upon us. Spare thou those, O God, who confess their faults. Restore thou those who are penitent; according to thy promises declared unto mankind in Christ Jesus our Lord. And grant, O most merciful Father, for his sake, that we may hereafter live a godly, righteous, and sober life, to the glory of thy holy Name. AMEN.[2]

POEM:

> Thine arm, O Lord, in days of old
> Was strong to heal and save;

It triumphed o'er disease and death,
  O'er darkness and the grave.
To thee they went, the blind, the dumb,
  The palsied and the lame,
The leper with his tainted life,
  The sick with fevered frame.

And lo, thy touch brought life and health,
  Gave speech, and strength, and sight;
And youth renewed and frenzy calmed
  Owned thee, the Lord of light:
And now, O Lord, be near to bless,
  Almighty as of yore,
In crowded street, by restless couch,
  As by Gennesereth's shore.

Be thou our great Deliverer still,
  Thou Lord of life and death;
Restore and quicken, soothe and bless
  With thine almighty breath:
To hands that work and eyes that see,
  Give wisdom's heavenly lore,
That whole and sick, and weak and strong,
  May praise thee evermore.

—Edward H. Plumptre

Hymn: "Saviour, Thy Dying Love."

Scripture:

I sought the Lord, and he heard me, and delivered me from all my fears.

Blessed is he whose transgression is forgiven, whose sin is covered.

Blessed is the man unto whom the Lord imputeth not iniquity, and in whose spirit there is no guile.[3]

Story of the Painting:

One of the most beautiful and pathetic chapters in Christ's life is the story of his relation to Mary Magdalene. The scripture account speaks of her as having once been possessed with seven devils. Just what that signifies in present-day medical terms we do not know; it may have been a physical ailment or some moral perversity. But the fact that the devils were seven rather than one indicates that she was sorely afflicted. There is no hint in the gospel story as to how the disease affected her conduct, but it has been customary to identify her with the "woman who was a sinner" in the account of the anointing in Simon's home. There are others who identify her with Mary, the sister of Martha and Lazarus.[4]

Whatever Mary's past may have been, after meeting Jesus, her one purpose was to minister to this prophet who had brought peace to her heart. She followed him from Magdala through Galilee, Samaria, and Judea, to Jerusalem. She was the last at the cross, the first at the grave. On Sunday morning she brought spices to the grave to perform her task of love in anointing the Master's body, and when she was robbed of this task her grief deprived her of the power to recognize his voice or form. Of the action of the two Marys at the cross, it has been said that the Magdalene's grief is the grief of a lover, while that of the other Mary is the unselfish love of a mother.

The place that Mary Magdalene occupies in Christian thought is not due, however, to her strange love for Jesus, but rather to what was wrought in her by Christ's love for her. It was Christ's love which delivered her from her past, and made her what she became. This is the center of interest in the Magdalene's life. This central fact the artist has seized upon and portrayed. He has represented in this picture the truth that it is possible to be delivered, through love, from the lowest depths, and lifted to the greatest heights. Whether Mary Magdalene and Mary of Bethany are the same or not, it is true that any Mary Magdalene can become a Mary of Bethany.

The Magdalene is an outstanding illustration of the great truth of human experience that "to whom much is forgiven, the same loveth much." We cannot be certain what Mary was delivered from, but it conditioned her love for Christ. She will always remain a striking example of the creative power of love. There is a tendency for love to idealize the object of its affection. By so doing it creates the hope and inspires the effort in the loved one to live up to that ideal. Christ's love led Mary to see in herself the possibilities which he saw in her. The man who feels as the Magdalene felt, that

> "All I could never be
> All men ignored in me,
> This I was worth to God,"

has the secret by which he will become other than what he is.

Love is said to be blind. No statement is more untrue, for nothing is so keen-eyed as love. Love is blind only in the sense that it deliberately shuts its eyes to defects, and centers its attention on the possibilities in order to help them grow and crowd out the defects. No other kind of love is worth having. Only so can one be delivered either from ignorance or from moral weakness; only so was the Magdalene delivered; only so can deliverance of any kind come. Man's contemplation of the possibilities which God's love sees in him is the greatest creative power in human life, for by it he is delivered from what he is, as the Magdalene was delivered, through the idealizing love of Jesus.[5]

LITANY OF SUPPLICATION:

Leader: Almighty God, our heavenly Father, from whom cometh every good and perfect gift, and without whom we cannot live at our best,

Group: Hear our prayer, we beseech thee.

Leader: O thou who takest away the sins of the world, we confess unto thee our shortcomings, our weaknesses, and our failures.

Group: We are heartily sorry for these sins.

Leader: O Lord, save us from low aim, indifference, false pride, and self-satisfaction,

Group: We beseech thee, O Lord.

Leader: For lack of purpose, half-heartedness in doing thy work, and disobedience to thy call,

Group: Forgive us, O Lord.

Leader: From unholy thoughts, impure motives, evil words or actions,

Group: Save us, O Lord.

Leader: From love of flattery, hasty utterances, and unkind words,

Group: Save us, O Lord.

Leader: Show us the paths wherein our feet should walk and give us the courage and determination to follow thy leading,

Group: We beseech thee, O Lord.

THE MAGDALENE

Leader: Purify our affections and bring us through the transforming power of love to the ideal which thou hast set for us,

Group: In Jesus' name. AMEN.

HYMN: "O Love That Wilt Not Let Me Go."

BENEDICTION:

> O Lord, and Master of us all,
>   Whate'er our name or sign,
> We own thy sway, we hear thy call,
>   We test our lives by thine. AMEN.
>   —JOHN G. WHITTIER

SERVICE 9

THE LOST SHEEP

(*Alfred Soord*)

AIM: To lead to a fresh insight into God's concern for every individual.

PRELUDE: Hymn tune "Sheltered Dale."

CALL TO WORSHIP:

> Shepherd of tender youth,
> Guiding in love and truth,
>   Through devious ways;
> Christ, our triumphant King,
> We come thy name to sing,
> Hither our children bring
>   To sound thy praise.
>
> Ever be thou our Guide,
> Our Shepherd and our pride,
>   Our staff and song;
> Jesus, thou Christ of God,
> By thy perennial word,
> Lead us where thou hast trod,
>   Make our faith strong.
>   —CLEMENT OF ALEXANDRIA

PRAYER:

O God, our Shepherd and our Guide, we come to thee in true humility asking forgiveness for all our sins. We confess our shortcomings before thee; have mercy upon us, pardon and deliver us from all our weaknesses. Create in us clean hearts and renew right spirits within us. Grant us the grace to overcome our faults; confirm and strengthen us that we may live daily before thee as worthy followers of thine. AMEN.

PRAYER RESPONSE:

> Father, hear the prayer we offer;
>   Not for ease that prayer shall be,
> But for strength, that we may ever
>   Live our lives courageously.
>
> Not forever in green pastures
>   Do we ask our way to be;
> But the steep and rugged pathway
>   May we tread rejoicingly.
>
> Be our strength in hours of weakness;
>   In our wanderings be our guide;
> Through endeavor, failure, danger,
>   Father, be thou at our side. AMEN.[1]
>   —LOVE M. WILLIS

UNISON SCRIPTURE READING:

I am the door; by me if any man enter in, he shall be saved, and shall go in and out, and find pasture. . . . I am come that they might have life, that they might have it more abundantly. I am the good shepherd: the good shepherd giveth his life for the sheep. . . . Other sheep I have, which are not of this fold: them also I must bring.

What man of you, having an hundred sheep, if he lose one of them, doth not leave the ninety and nine in the wilderness, and go after that which is lost, until he find it?

And when he hath found it, he layeth it on his shoulders, rejoicing. And when he cometh home, he calleth together his friends and neighbors, saying unto them, Rejoice with me; for I have found my sheep which was lost.

When Jesus saw the multitudes, he was moved with compassion on them, because they fainted, and were scattered abroad, as sheep having no shepherd.

And when he had called unto him his twelve disciples . . . . he said, Go to the lost sheep of the house of Israel. And as ye go, preach, saying, The kingdom of heaven is at hand.[2]

PAINTINGS

Hymn: "The Lord Is My Shepherd," or
    "Saviour, Like a Shepherd Lead Us."

Poem:

> There's not a bird with lonely nest,
> In pathless wood or mountain crest,
> Nor meaner thing, which does not share,
> O God, in thy paternal care.
>
> Each barren crag, each desert rude,
> Holds thee within its solitude;
> And thou dost bless the wanderer there,
> Who makes his solitary prayer.
>
> In busy mart and crowded street,
> No less than in the still retreat,
> Thou, Lord, art near, our souls to bless,
> With all a father's tenderness.
>
> And we, where'er our lot is cast,
> While life, and thought, and feeling last,
> Through all the years, in every place,
> Will bless thee for thy boundless grace.
> —Baptist W. Noel

Interpretation of the Painting:

The theme of the Good Shepherd has been handled over and over again, but usually one sees the same type of picture, the figure of a well-dressed man holding a lamb in his arms. To one who has seen the shepherds in Palestine there is something particularly repugnant in such a picture. No real shepherd ever wore the elegant draperies that adorn these artists' models. No real shepherd ever sported such curls or posed so gracefully, or showed such an absence of character in his face.

On the contrary, when you come upon a real shepherd in the shepherd's country, something is apt to grip your heart and your throat. Shepherding there is a man's job! There you see the rough jacket made of a fleece turned wool-side in; the bare bronzed chest, the bare legs scratched with thorns, the rough shoes of rawhide, the great club of oak, heavy enough to fell a bear; the high-stepping stride and the

THE LOST SHEEP, by Alfred Soord

THE HOPE OF THE WORLD, by Harold Copping

THE LOST SHEEP

muscles like steel that endure the tramps over rocky country. The
light in the eye and the absence of fear point to the fact that the shepherd has often faced danger alone. As a rule, you will see a lamb in
his arms. Such a shepherd is the person that Jesus had in mind when
he said, "I am the good Shepherd."

Soord has caught the spirit of the original story which Jesus told
of the Lost Sheep. This is a parable of rescue; the sheep is lost. No
careful shepherd would have led his flock into such a pasture as this;
the foolish sheep herself is responsible for the situation. It may have
been too much wandering, or sheer carelessness, or she may have
fallen to this point. Whatever the cause, here she is, clinging to the
edge of the cliff, unable to move, with the great canyon below and
the hungry eagles drawing nearer and nearer to their prey. Night is
coming on and a storm is threatening.[3]

At this particular moment, when the sheep has reached its ex-
tremity, the good shepherd comes upon the scene. He has picked his
way down the cliff, inch by inch, at the risk of his life. Supporting
himself by means of the shepherd's crook fastened into the rocky ledge,
he reaches out for the lamb. He exhibits such strength and determination that we believe he would be able to cope with any situation.
No night could ever be so dark, or the storm so fierce that he would
not continue to search until he found the sheep.

Jesus called himself the Good Shepherd who came "to seek and to
save that which was lost" and is not willing that "even the least of
these shall perish." He searches just as diligently for the poor, the
outcast, the unfortunate; no one strays beyond the outreach of his love.
The artist has pictured the moment when the sheep is found, and we
feel the joy of the Master as he says, "Rejoice with me, for I have
found my sheep."

SPECIAL MUSIC: "The Ninety and Nine."

LITANY OF SUPPLICATION:

Leader: O God, our Father, thou Searcher of our hearts and lives, we
draw near to thee in meekness and humility.

Group: Grant unto us an awareness of thy presence.

Leader: We acknowledge and confess our unworthiness.

Group: Have mercy upon us, O Lord.

Leader: O thou, who takest away the sins of the world, save us from the sin of low desires, from contentment with things as they are.

Group: Have mercy upon us, O Lord.

Leader: Hear our prayer of confession and pardon our unwillingness to follow the visions which have come to us.

Group: Have mercy upon us, O Lord.

Leader: Stir up within us a desire to fight against the sins of ignorance, selfishness, and lack of purpose.

Group: Hear our prayer, we beseech thee.

Leader: Forgive us for lack of patience, nervous haste, and shameless neglect of our opportunities.

Group: Hear our prayer, we beseech thee.

Leader: Forgive our selfish desires, our indifference, our lack of vision.

Group: Hear our prayer, we beseech thee.

Leader: Help us to make our wills entirely thine and co-operate with thee in thy purpose for our lives.

Group: In Jesus' name. AMEN.

HYMN:

> Gracious Spirit, dwell with us;
> We ourselves would gracious be;
> And with words that help and heal
> Would thy life in ours reveal;
> And with actions bold and meek
> Would for Christ our Saviour speak.
>
> Truthful Spirit, dwell in us;
> We ourselves would truthful be;
> And with wisdom kind and clear
> Let thy life in ours appear;
> And with actions brotherly
> Speak our Lord's sincerity.
>
> Silent Spirit, dwell with us;
> We ourselves would quiet be;

THE LOST SHEEP

Quiet as the growing blade,
Which through earth its way hath made
Silently, like morning light,
Putting mists and chills to flight.

Mighty Spirit, dwell with us;
We ourselves would mighty be;
Mighty so as to prevail
Where unaided man must fail;
Ever by a mighty hope,
Pressing on and bearing up.

Holy Spirit, dwell with us;
We ourselves would holy be;
Separate from sin, we would
Choose and cherish all things good,
And whatever we can be
Give to him who gave us thee! [4]
                    —Thomas Toke Lynch

BENEDICTION:

May the goodness and the mercy of the Lord follow us all the
days of our lives. Amen.

SERVICE 10

THE HOPE OF THE WORLD

(Harold Copping)

Aim: To lead the group to realize that since God is the Father of all
races he would have us show a real concern for all his children

Prelude: Hymn tune "Canonbury."

Call to Worship:

O come, let us worship and bow down: let us kneel before the
Lord our Maker.

I have loved the habitation of thy house. This is none other than
the house of God, and this is the gate to heaven.

Hymn: "Lift Up Your Hearts," or
"Jesus Shall Reign."

Responsive Reading:

Leader: Lift up your heads, O ye gates; and be ye lifted up, ye everlasting doors; and the King of glory shall come in.

Group: Who is this King of glory? The Lord strong and mighty
the Lord mighty in battle.

Leader: Lift up your heads, O ye gates; even lift them up, ye ever
lasting doors; and the King of glory shall come in.

Group: Who is this King of glory? The Lord of hosts, he is the
King of glory.

Leader: Lift up your hearts.

Group: We lift them up unto the Lord.

THE HOPE OF THE WORLD

Leader: O Lord, open thou our eyes.

Group: That we may behold wondrous things out of thy law.

Leader: O Lord, open thou our lips.

Group: And our mouth shall show forth thy praise.

Leader: Praise ye the Lord.

Group: The Lord's name be praised.

Leader: From the rising of the sun to the going down of the same, the Lord's name is to be praised.

Group: O that men would praise the Lord for his goodness, and for his wonderful works to the children of men.[1]

Prayer:

O God, our Father, we rejoice that we can come to thee in confidence and in trust. We realize that every child is a member of thy great family. Help us to have a Christian attitude toward the children of all races. Lead us into a new meaning of the worth of human life. Grant that in our upward climb together we may learn how to live as brothers with all races of men. Amen.

Poem:

At length there dawns the glorious day
  By prophets long foretold;
At length the chorus clearer grows
  That shepherds heard of old.
The day of dawning brotherhood
  Breaks on our eager eyes,
And human hatreds flee before
  The radiant eastern skies.

For what are sundering strains of blood,
  Or ancient caste and creed?
One claim unites all men in God
  To serve each human need.
Then here together, brother men,
  We pledge the Lord anew
Our loyal love, our stalwart faith,
  Our service strong and true.

PAINTINGS

One common faith unites us all,
  We seek one common goal,
One tender comfort broods upon
  The struggling human soul.
To this clear call of brotherhood
  Our hearts responsive ring;
We join the glorious new crusade
  Of our great Lord and King.
                    —OZORA S. DAVIS

OFFERTORY: "Traumerei" by Schumann.

Leader: Remember the words of the Lord Jesus, how he said, it is
    more blessed to give than to receive. Let your light so shine
    before men, that they may see your good works and glorify
    your Father which is in heaven.

Group: All things come of thee, O Lord, and of thine own have we
    given thee. AMEN.

SCRIPTURE:

And they brought unto him also infants, that he would touch them:
but when his disciples saw it, they rebuked them. But Jesus called
them unto him, and said, Suffer little children to come unto me, and
forbid them not: for of such is the kingdom of God.[2]

INTERPRETATION OF THE PAINTING:

Harold Copping, a contemporary English artist, has given one of
the most satisfying pictures of Jesus in the painting "The Hope of the
World." Jesus is shown as the children's friend as he gathers them
about him. Each child is happy in the love of the new-found friend,
and on each face is seen the simple trust of a child. The artist is
trying to show what Jesus meant when he said, "Except ye become as
little children ye shall in no wise enter the kingdom of heaven." By
this statement "Jesus did not mean to place innocence above virtue,
helplessness above strength, ignorance above wisdom, or inexperience
and immaturity above ripened and disciplined years. But he is saying
that the first step of the Christian life is loving and trusting as a little
child. The noblest character is he who can look the universe full in
the face and still trust—trust as absolutely as a child. To do this is to
live by faith—to be religious." [3]

THE HOPE OF THE WORLD

The artist is showing a symbolic grouping of the races in this picture. He did not attempt to paint the children of all of the countries of the world, but is showing one of each of the major races— the yellow, red, black, brown, and white. The dainty little Indian girl is sitting gracefully on Jesus' knee, and beside him stands the white girl with Jesus' arm encircling her. The little brown girl and the Chinese lad are leaning on his knee and gazing intently into his face. The absorbed expression on the face of the Chinese lad leads us to believe that the Master is answering a question which the lad has asked.

All of the children are touching Jesus except the negro boy who sits at his feet. Yet the artist has given him the most prominent place in the picture. One can neither overlook him, nor miss the beauty of his sturdy form, nor his intense interest in what the Master is saying to the Chinese lad. The children do not resent one another, but they seem to feel that each one has a perfect right to be there, and we believe that Jesus would not have them otherwise. The white girl has her hand on the shoulder of the Indian girl, and Jesus' arms encircle them all except the child at his feet.

The expression on Jesus face indicates sympathy, love, and understanding for the children. He is as near to any of them as he is to all; his love and tender solicitude include them all. The artist, by portraying the sturdy, racial beauty of each child, is showing that Jesus is pleased with the individual differences and with the variety of gifts which the children have to offer. Aggrey of Africa in his parable of piano keys said, "You can play a tune of sorts on the white keys; you can play a tune of sorts on the black keys; but for harmony you must use both black and white." The artist is conveying this message which is contained in the invitation of Jesus to the children of all races to come unto him, for he is the hope of the world when he becomes enthroned in the heart and life of the children of all the world.

PRAYER:

O God, our Father, thou who hast made of one blood all nations of men to dwell on the face of the earth, and who didst send thy Son into the world to seek and to save, hear us as we pray for the people of all nations. We thank thee for the privilege of being fellow-workers with thee through our offerings. Touch our hearts that we may see the need and do our part in bringing thy kingdom on earth.

Be thou very near to those who are carrying on thy work in the various fields. Strengthen their faith and give them the assurance of thy presence in their lives. Give us a greater desire to support them by our prayers and by our offerings. In the Name of Christ, our Lord. AMEN.

POEM:

> Of all the gifts the gods bestow,
> The greatest gift we humans know,
> The sweetest joy, the highest good
> Of life itself is brotherhood.
>
> From whence has come this wonder thing,
> This rich reward for clown and king?
> How shall we know the password, pray,
> When comrade Christ shall come our way?
>
> True brotherhood is comradeship
> Of heart and soul and life and lip;
> True comradeship by day and night
> With brown and yellow, black and white.[4]
>
> —WILLIAM L. STIDGER

HYMN: "O Zion, Haste," or
"Lead On, O King Eternal."

BENEDICTION:

Grant that grace, mercy, and peace abide in our hearts now and forevermore. AMEN.

SERVICE 11

THE HEALER

(Harold Copping)

Aim: To lead to a greater desire to share the good news of the gospel with all races.

Prelude: Hymn tune "Antioch."

Call to Worship:

> O sing unto the Lord a new song;
> Sing unto the Lord, all the earth.
> Sing unto the Lord, bless his name;
> Show forth his salvation from day to day.

Hymn: "We've a Story to Tell to the Nations," or
"O Brother Man, Fold to Thy Heart."

Responsive Reading:

Leader: Jesus said: Go ye therefore, and teach all nations; teaching them to observe all things whatsoever I have commanded you.

Group: (to be sung)

> Christ for the world we sing!
> The world to Christ we bring,
>   With loving zeal;
> The poor, and them that mourn,
> The faint and overborne,
> Sin-sick and sorrow-worn,
>   Whom Christ doth heal.

Leader: The Lord is not willing that any should perish, but that all should come to repentance.

Group:
> Christ for the world we sing!
> The world to Christ we bring,
>> With fervent prayer;
> The wayward and the lost,
> By restless passions tossed,
> Redeemed at countless cost,
>> From dark despair.

Leader: The Son of Man is come to seek and to save that which was lost.

Group:
> Christ for the world we sing!
> The world to Christ we bring,
>> With one accord;
> With us the work to share,
> With us reproach to dare,
> With us the cross to bear,
>> For Christ our Lord.

Leader: And, lo, I am with you alway, even unto the end of the world.

Group:
> Christ for the world we sing!
> The world to Christ we bring,
>> With joyful song;
> The new-born souls, whose days,
> Reclaimed from error's ways,
> Inspired with hope and praise,
>> To Christ belong.[1]

PRAYER:

O God, thou who hast made of one blood all nations to dwell together on the face of the earth, and didst send thy Son to seek and to save the lost; grant that we may share thy gospel with those who know it not. Thou who dost love thy children everywhere, fill us with a desire for the salvation of all men. As the Master sent forth his disciples to tell the story of redeeming love, grant that we may feel a responsibility to send the message to those who have not heard the gospel. In Jesus' name. AMEN.

HYMN: "Lift up Our Hearts."

THE HEALER

Harold Copping, the English artist, has transferred to canvas an incident in the life of a Christian doctor serving in the heart of Africa. He has caught the spirit of the medical missionaries as they have gone into the darkest continents carrying their ministry of healing. He may have been inspired by the work of his own countryman, Livingstone, or by a present-day follower of Christ ministering to the needy in the far corners of the earth. He has given us a glimpse into the life of one whose name might well be added to the list of heroes given in the eleventh chapter of Hebrews.

In the background of this picture may be seen the dense foliage of tropical Africa. To the right are the thatched roofs of native huts almost hidden by the luxuriant growth. In the foreground the medical missionary is kneeling; beside him are the case of surgical instruments and the metal box of prepared medicines. A low stool and two earthen vessels containing water for the cleansing of wounds complete the equipment. The doctor is holding in his hand the medicine which he is preparing to give to the sick lad before him.

It is not difficult to fill in the scene which is being enacted on the canvas. Two African boys and a mother with her child have come for help. It may be that the mother had been to the witch-doctor and failed to secure aid for the child who had grown steadily worse. At any rate, he is now unable to sit up; and the mother, kneeling beside him, supports him as the doctor gives him the medicine. Aid has just been given to the other boys, as may be seen by the bandages. They are standing at the right, watching intently, reluctant to leave. The younger of them is delighted at the response of the sick lad, who opens his eyes as the medicine begins to have the desired effect. There is an expression of sympathy and understanding on the face of the doctor, who is oblivious to everything except the reaction of the sick child.

To these children of the wilderness the doctor is more than a healer; he is a miracle worker. But a far greater healer is seen in Christ, the Great Physician, in the background of the picture. The artist is portraying the message that it was Christ, the Healer, who led the doctor to go to Africa to bring the aid of medicine to the needy savages. He is also saying that the Spirit of Christ is watching over the doctor, guiding his hand, imparting strength and skill to aid in the task of healing. This is the artist's way of interpreting the scripture, "Lo, I am with you alway, even unto the end of the world." Christ's promise is here fulfilled as it has been many times. Wherever the doctor goes he has the assurance that he is not going in his own strength and that he is not left alone.[2]

It is not an easy matter to be a doctor to primitive people. There is constant anxiety about the patients who have undergone operations because they will not do as they are told. If they feel inclined, they bathe in the river the day after the operation, unconcerned about the danger of infection. If a man has been asked to abstain from food, when he becomes tired of fasting, he secretly enjoys an ample meal which he has implored his wife to prepare for him.

Many of the patients come from such a distance that they arrive half starved and in such condition that it requires weeks of nursing before the doctor can venture to operate. The people from the interior have first to undertake a long march to reach the river. Having no craft of their own, they must wait until a boat passes in which there is room for them. When the patient recovers, there is the problem of returning him to his home, and also the anxiety lest he not be able to survive the hardships of the journey.

In case of a death at the hospital, the doctor tries to explain the cause to the relatives, but they are accustomed to ascribe the death of a person to the influence of magic exercised against him. In most cases they begin a search for the one whom they believe to be responsible for the evil magic. And the innocent victim of this cruel superstition loses his life in a staged accident or is poisoned. The stamping out of the work of the witch-doctor is difficult. Most of the natives keep to themselves what they know about a witch-doctor, for fear of their own lives.

As a result of the belief in taboos and curses, the natives, when they reach the hospital, are in a pathetic state of distress. But most of them believe that the taboos, curses, and magic are without effect on the land of the Mission Station and the hospital. Anyone who has penetrated into the imaginary world of primitive people, and knows something of the fears in which they live, can no longer doubt that it is the duty of the medical missionary to liberate them from these superstitions, as well as to minister to them in illness.[3]

> By the roads that wound uphill and down,
>   Beside the lake in Galilee,
> From house to house, from town to town,
>   Our Lord fulfilled his ministry.

THE HEALER

How blest the homes that knew him then;
 And holy yet the paths he trod!
O gracious heart that loved all men!
 O patient feet that walked with God.[4]

—Louis F. Benson

PRAYER:

Our Father, Giver of every good and perfect gift, endow with wisdom those who teach and heal, and grant that they may look unto thee, the Source of all wisdom. With thy aid no task is too difficult. Strengthen them that they may venture all things for thee. We thank thee for the privilege of being fellow-workers with thee through our offerings. Open our hearts that we may see the continuing need and do our part in answering it. We ask thy continued blessing on those who carry thy ministry of healing into the needy corners of the world. Give them an increase in faith, enrich their lives, and be thou ever very near them. Grant us the grace to be fellow-workers with them by our prayers and by our offerings. Make us ever ready to use our talents in building thy kingdom. Pour out thy spirit upon all people, bring all races into thy fold, and hasten the coming of thy kingdom. In Jesus' name, we pray. AMEN.

POEM:

O Lord, thy benediction give
 On all who teach, on all who learn,
That so thy Church may holier live,
 And every lamp more brightly burn.

Give those that learn the willing ear,
 The spirit meek, the guileless mind;
Such gifts will make the lowliest here
 Far better than a kingdom find.

O bless the shepherd, bless the sheep,
 That guide and guided both be one;
One in the faithful watch they keep,
 One in the joy of work well done.

—John Armstrong

HYMN: "The Light of God Is Falling," or
   "O Zion, Haste."

BENEDICTION:

Now unto him that is able to do exceedingly abundantly above all that we ask or think, according to the power that worketh in us, be glory for ever and ever. AMEN.

SERVICE 12

THE PRESENCE

(*A. E. Borthwick*)

Aim: To lead to a fresh insight into the importance of bringing an attitude of sincerity and humility into our worship.

Prelude: "Prelude in A Major," by Chopin (Opus 28, No. 7).

Call to Worship:

> Every morning mercies new
> Fall as fresh as morning dew;
> Every morning let us pay
> Tribute with the early day:
> For thy mercies, Lord, are sure,
> Thy compassion doth endure.
>
> Let our prayers each morn prevail,
> That these gifts may never fail;
> And, as we confess the sin
> And the tempter's power within,
> Every morning, for the strife,
> Feed us with the bread of life.
> —Greville Phillimore

Hymn: "Another Day Is Dawning," or
"Still, Still with Thee."

Responsive Reading:

Leader: O Lord, thou hast searched me, and known me.

Group: Thou knowest my downsitting and mine uprising; thou understandest my thought afar off.

Leader: Thou compassest my path and my lying down, and are acquainted with all my ways.

Group: For there is not a word in my tongue, but, lo, O Lord, thou knowest it altogether.

Leader: Thou hast beset me behind and before, and laid thine hand upon me.

Group: Such knowledge is too wonderful for me; it is high, I cannot attain unto it.

Leader: Whither shall I go from thy Spirit? or whither shall I flee from thy presence?

Group: If I take the wings of the morning, and dwell in the uttermost parts of the sea; even there shall thy hand lead me, and thy right hand shall hold me.

Leader: If I say, Surely the darkness shall cover me; even the night shall be light about me.

Group: Yea, the darkness hideth not from thee; but the night shineth as the day: the darkness and the light are both alike to thee.

Leader: Such knowledge is too wonderful for me; it is high, I cannot attain unto it.

Group: How precious also are thy thoughts unto me, O God! how great is the sum of them! If I should count them, they are more in number than the sand: when I awake, I am still with thee.[1]

Prayer:

Our Father, direct us, in all our doings, with thy most gracious favor, and further us with thy continual help; that in all our works begun, continued, and ended in thee, may we glorify thy Holy Name, and finally, by thy mercy, obtain everlasting life, through Jesus Christ, our Lord. Amen.[2]

Hymn:

Spirit of Life, in this new dawn,
Give us the faith that follows on,

THE PRESENCE

Letting thine all-pervading power
Fulfill the dream of this high hour.

Spirit Creative, give us light,
Lifting the raveled mists of night.
Touch thou our dust with spirit hand
And make us souls that understand.

Spirit Redeeming, give us grace
When crucified to seek thy face,
To read forgiveness in thine eyes—
Today with thee in Paradise.

Spirit Consoling, let us find
Thy hand when sorrows leave us blind
In the gray valley let us hear
Thy silent voice: "Lo, I am near."

Spirit of Love, at evening-time,
When weary feet refuse to climb,
Give us thy vision, eyes that see,
Beyond the dark, the dawn and thee.[3]

—EARL MARLATT

OFFERING.

OFFERING RESPONSE:

Bless thou the gifts our hands have brought:
  Bless thou the work our hearts have planned;
Ours is the faith, the will the thought;
  The rest, O God, is in thy hand. AMEN.

—SAMUEL LONGFELLOW

POEM:

O thou, in all thy might so far,
  In all thy love so near,
Beyond the range of sun and star,
  And yet beside us here:

What heart can comprehend thy name,
  Or searching find thee out

—81—

Who art within, a quickening Flame,
    A Presence round about.

Yet though I know thee but in part,
    I ask not, Lord, for more;
Enough for me to know thou art,
    To love thee and adore.
            —FREDERICK L. HOSMER

SCRIPTURE:

Ask, and it shall be given you; seek, and ye shall find; knock, and it shall be opened unto you.[4]

INTERPRETATION OF THE PAINTING:

Borthwick in "The Presence" has given a painting which does not yield its full message at first glance. He has painted the interior of a great cathedral which is dimly lighted except for two spots of light. He has shown the pomp and glory, the dignity and beauty appropriate to such a scene. As we study the picture, our attention is directed to the bright spot around the pulpit. Although the light is so brilliant that it almost dazzles, it does not seem to come from the windows, but from some unseen source. The other light in the foreground comes from the figure of Christ standing in the rear of the building.

As our eyes become accustomed to the dimly lighted church, the details are more noticeable. In this Gothic structure, with its high ceiling and wide arches, the congregation has assembled for worship. A handful of people may be seen near the altar. The larger light illuminates the altar, revealing the elements on the communion table; and the choir may be seen on the raised floor of the chancel. The minister officiates while the people participate in the ritual service.

But why the lonely, kneeling figure crouching behind the last pew, almost hidden in the shadows? Not daring to mingle with the other worshipers, too conscious of sin, perhaps, to venture near the altar, she kneels in penitence near the door. Her clasped hands above her head are the only detail which the artist gives of her. Perhaps she hopes that no one will discover her as she prays. We do not know the burden of her prayer; but "The Presence" comes, and her prayer is answered. How gentle and tender is the gesture of Christ's hand

THE PRESENCE

...ng, and how quieting to the troubled heart of the

...re surprised that Christ is shown in the rear of the
...f at the altar where the minister is officiating, or
...rs as they take part in the service. None of them is
...nce except the penitent woman in the rear. The
...the thought that regardless of elaborate building,
...tual or other ceremony, Christ reveals himself to
...him in an attitude of deep humility. Always he
...known to those who ask and seek his presence, whether
...the great cathedral, the home, the crowded streets, or the solitude
...f the out-of-doors.

POEM:

> I met God in the morning
>   When my day was at its best;
> And his Presence came like sunrise
>   With a glory in my breast.
>
> All day long the Presence lingered,
>   All day long he stayed with me;
> And we sailed in perfect calmness
>   O'er a very troubled sea.
>
> Other ships were blown and battered,
>   Other ships were sore distressed,
> But the winds that seemed to drive them,
>   Brought to us both peace and rest.
>
> Then I thought of other mornings,
>   With a keen remorse of mind,
> When I, too, had loosed the moorings,
>   With the Presence left behind.
>
> So I think I know the secret,
>   Learned from many a troubled way;
> You must seek him in the morning,
>   If you want him through the day.[5]
>   —RALPH S. CUSHMAN

PRAYER:

O thou Revealer of Truth and Judge of men's motives, we come to thee in all sincerity asking for a revelation of thyself. As we meditate on the life of Christ which gives us a vision of thee, help us to test our own lives by his example. As we bring to thee our burdens, our disappointments, our frustrations, grant us thy peace. If we are anxious or troubled, give us the patience which comes through faith in thy promises. If others have wronged us, help us to forgive freely. If the future seems dark, give us greater hope and confidence. If easily discouraged, give us greater courage. Help us never to swerve from the convictions which we believe to be right, and may we strive to make those high and holy visions which come from thee a reality in our lives. AMEN.

SERVICE 13

THE LIGHT OF THE WORLD

(*Holman Hunt*)

AIM: To lead to a clearer conception of the value of Christ's presence in one's life.

PRELUDE: Hymn tune "Passion Chorale."

CALL TO WORSHIP:

> Jesus, thou Joy of loving hearts!
>   Thou Fount of life! Thou Light of men!
> From the blest bliss that earth imparts,
>   We turn unfilled to thee again.
>
> O Jesus, ever with us stay;
>   Make all our moments calm and bright;
> Chase the dark night of sin away,
>   Shed o'er the world thy holy light!
>   —BERNARD OF CLAIRVAUX

HYMN: "O Grant Us Light, That We May Know," or
    "There's a Stranger at the Door," or
    "I Gave My Life for Thee."

UNISON PRAYER:

Almighty God, unto whom all hearts are open, all desires known, and from whom no secrets are hid; cleanse the thoughts of our hearts by the inspiration of thy Holy Spirit, that we may perfectly love thee and worthily magnify thy Holy Name.[1] O thou who art ever knocking at the door of our hearts, help us to respond to thee. We would

— 85 —

open our hearts to thee at all times. Fill us with thy Holy Spirit, for we realize that thou hast created us for thyself and we will not rest until we have found thee. Come into our lives and abide with us forever. AMEN.

RESPONSIVE READING:

Leader: In the beginning was the Word, and the Word was with God, and the Word was God.

Group: The same was in the beginning with God.

Leader: All things were made by him; and without him was not any thing made that was made.

Group: In him was life; and the life was the light of men.

Leader: And the light shineth in darkness; and the darkness comprehended it not.

Group: There was a man sent from God, whose name was John.

Leader: The same came for a witness, to bear witness of the Light, that all men through him might believe.

Group: He was not that Light, but was sent to bear witness of that Light.

Leader: That was the true Light, which lighteth every man that cometh into the world.

Group: He was in the world, and the world was made by him, and the world knew him not.

Leader: He came unto his own, and his own received him not.

Group: But as many as received him, to them gave he power to become the sons of God, even to them that believe on his name:

Leader: Which were born, not of blood, nor of the will of the flesh, nor of the will of man, but of God.

Group: And the Word was made flesh, and dwelt among us, and we beheld his glory, the glory as of the only begotten of the Father, full of grace and truth.

Leader: John bare witness of him, and cried, saying, This was he of whom I spake, He that cometh after me is preferred before me: for he was before me.

THE LIGHT OF THE WORLD

Group: And of his fulness have all we received, and grace for grace.[2]

PoEM:

Light of the world, we hail thee,
  Flushing the eastern skies;
Never shall darkness veil thee
  Again from human eyes;
Too long, alas, withholden,
  Now spread from shore to shore;
Thy light, so glad and golden,
  Shall set on earth no more.

Light of the world, thy beauty
  Steals into every heart,
And glorifies with duty
  Life's poorest, humblest part;
Thou robest in thy splendor
  The simplest ways of men,
And helpest them to render
  Light back to thee again.

Light of the world, illumine
  This darkened earth of thine,
Till everything that's human
  Be filled with what's divine;
Till every tongue and nation,
  From sin's dominion free,
Rise in the new creation
  Which springs from love and thee.
          —JOHN S. B. MONSELL

INTERPRETATION OF THE PAINTING:

Holman Hunt's painting, "The Light of the World," completed in 1854, created quite a sensation. For the first time a picture became the subject of conversation in England from one end of the island to the other. It was shown in London and throughout the British Isles. Hundreds of thousands of copies were sold.

Before the artist painted this picture he spent months traveling in Palestine studying scenery, types, and costumes in order that he might have the correct background; and he has produced a masterpiece, accurate in every detail. There is not one false note in the entire picture. Its beauty rests in its exquisite coloring, and the message is portrayed by its significant symbolism.

The legend beneath the picture is the verse of Scripture, "Behold, I stand at the door and knock." The picture appeared at a time of awakening in the political and industrial world, and appealed to the people because of the timely message which it brought. To some of the leaders it represented Christ knocking at the door of the Church, which seemed to them closed to the Spirit of God. The artist was, of course, sensitive to the condition of the Church at that time, but he intended to convey a message to the individual as well.

The moment selected for the painting of the picture is when the call of Christ comes and a decision must be made. It is easy to see that the door represents the door of the heart and that it has not been opened in a long time. It is fast barred, and streaks of rust stain the wood below its hinges. It is knitted and bound by creeping tendrils of ivy. The weeds have grown up in front of it and have gone to seed. A bat, the symbol of darkness, is startled by the lights and flutters out from beneath the eaves of the house where it has been making its home. The threshold is overgrown with brambles and nettles. But there is something still more significant about the door—there is no latchstring. It cannot be opened from without. There is only one way to enter—it must be opened from within.

Jesus is wearing the white robe of the prophet, around his shoulders is the mantle of the priest, and upon his head, the crown of gold. The artist is showing Christ in his office of prophet, priest, and king. There are two crowns upon his head—one, an eternal crown, placed there by his Father, signifying his right to rule; the other, a crown of thorns, placed there by his enemies as a token of hate and a badge of suffering. However, the thorns have lost their sharpness, having put forth leaves, showing that love conquers hate.

There are three lights in the picture. The light of conscience, carried by Christ, reveals sin as it shines upon the weeds and the door which has long been closed. The second light comes from the background in the first faint rays of the dawn of the new day, representing the dawn of a new life that comes when Christ enters. The third light is the light about the head of Christ, representing the abundant life which he brings.

When the picture first appeared there were some who objected to the lantern in the hand of Christ. They asked, "Why should the Light of the World go around carrying a lantern?" The artist is trying to bring to our attention the fact that when Christ enters a human heart, he not only throws light upon sin, but he brings new life when the door of the heart is opened and he is allowed to enter.

This painting has had the greatest effect of any painting of recent times. There is the same appeal to every generation. Christ is standing at the door of the heart of each one of us seeking admittance. There is tenderness and love shown in the expression of his face. He is knocking patiently, but he will not batter down the door. Traveling by night he has reached the door by dawn in order that we may fare forth with him in time to see the loveliness of the day breaking. Although the journey may bring hardship, suffering or danger, it will also bring companionship with Christ. Will we open the door, accepting the new life which he offers, or will we refuse to open it and miss the companionship with him?

Hymn:

O Jesus, thou art standing
　　Outside the fast-closed door,
In lowly patience waiting
　　To pass the threshold o'er:
Shame on us, Christian brethren,
　　His name and sign who bear,
O shame, thrice shame upon us;
　　To keep him standing there!

O Jesus, thou art knocking:
　　And lo, that hand is scarred,
And thorns thy brow encircle,
　　And tears thy face have marred.
O love that passeth knowledge,
　　So patiently to wait!
O sin that hath no equal,
　　So fast to bar the gate!

O Jesus, thou art pleading
　　In accents meek and low,
"I died for you, my children,
　　And will ye treat me so?"

—89—

O Lord, with shame and sorrow
We open now the door;
Dear Saviour, enter, enter,
And leave us nevermore.
—WILLIAM WALSHAM HOW

LITANY OF SUPPLICATION:

Leader: O God, thou art very great; thou art clothed with honor and with majesty. Thou coverest thyself with light as with a garment.

Group: We magnify thy name, O Lord.

Leader: Thou art the light of all men; thou art our light and our salvation.

Group: Shed thy light into these hearts of ours.

Leader: Our Father, if we have preferred the darkness to the light,

Group: Forgive our foolish ways.

Leader: If we have neglected to pray and have permitted sin to creep into our lives,

Group: Forgive us, we pray.

Leader: If we have followed thee blindly, refusing to obey thy will,

Group: Forgive us, we beseech thee.

Leader: It is thee and not thy gifts that we crave. Enter our lives and dwell there forever,

Group: We beseech thee, O Lord.

Leader: We would live, not for self, but for thee. Lead us into the abundant life which thou dost offer,

Group: We beseech thee, O Lord. In Jesus' name. AMEN.

BENEDICTION:

May thy Holy Spirit guide us as we go forth to live a new life. AMEN.

PART TWO

SCULPTURE

SERVICE 14

THE HAND OF GOD
(*Auguste Rodin*)

AIM: To lead to a clearer conception of God through his creative work.

PRELUDE: Hymn tune "Creation" (Haydn).

CALL TO WORSHIP:

> Holy, Holy, Holy! Lord God Almighty!
> Early in the morning our song shall rise to thee;
> Holy, Holy, Holy, merciful and mighty!
> God in Three Persons, blessed Trinity.

UNISON RESPONSE:

Let the words of our mouths and the meditation of our hearts be acceptable in thy sight, O Lord, our strength and our redeemer. AMEN.

HYMN: "The Spacious Firmament on High," or
"Praise the Lord! Ye Heavens, Adore Him."

RESPONSIVE READING:

Leader: Holy holy, holy is the Lord of hosts; the whole earth is full of his glory.

Group: Glory and honor are in his presence: strength and gladness are in his place.

Leader: Give unto the Lord the glory due unto his name: worship the Lord in the beauty of holiness.

Group: O magnify the Lord with me, and let us exalt his name together.

Leader: Great and marvelous are thy works, Lord God Almighty; just and true are thy ways, thou King of the ages.

Group: O Lord, our Lord, how excellent is thy name in all the earth! who hast set thy glory above the heavens.

Leader: O come, let us worship and bow down: let us kneel before the Lord our Maker.[1]

UNISON READING:

The heavens declare thy glory,
The firmament thy power;
Day unto day the story
Repeats from hour to hour;
Night unto night replying,
Proclaims in every land,
O Lord, with voice undying,
The wonders of thy hand.

The sun with royal splendor
Goes forth to chant thy praise
And moonbeams soft and tender
Their gentler anthem raise:
O'er every tribe and nation
The music strange is poured;
The song of all creation
To thee, creation's Lord.

All heaven on high rejoices
To do its Maker's will;
The stars with solemn voices
Resound thy praises still:
So let my whole behavior,
Thoughts, words, and actions be,
O Lord, my Strength, my Saviour,
One ceaseless song to thee.

—THOMAS R. BIRKS

THE HAND OF GOD

SCRIPTURE:

In the beginning God created the heaven and the earth. And the earth was without form, and void; and darkness was upon the face of the deep. And the spirit of God moved upon the face of the waters. And God said, Let there be light: and there was light. . . . . And God said, Let us make man in our image, after our likeness; and let them have dominion over the fish of the sea, and over the fowl of the air, and over the cattle, and over all the earth, and over every creeping thing that creepeth upon the earth. So God created man in his own image, in the image of God created he him; male and female created he them. And God blessed them, and God said unto them, Be fruitful, and multiply, and replenish the earth, and subdue it: and have dominion over the fish of the sea, and over the fowl of the air, and over every living thing that moveth upon the earth. . . . And God saw everything that he had made, and behold, it was very good.[2]

POEM:

I heard God speak this day
Along an Alpine way.
'Twas where a mountain shower
Had washed a crimson flower
Nodding in the blue heights
When the rain was through.
It bent as if in prayer
Beneath the rain-washed air.
'Twas when the sun came out
I thought I heard God shout
With laughter down the seams
And crevices and streams.
I thought I saw His face
In one high, holy place
Up close against the sky
Where stars and planets fly;
Up where the clouds lie low
And wind tides ebb and flow;
From which I heard Him speak
In whispers of the wind
Some words supremely kind.

SCULPTURE

'Twas this I heard God speak
Through a flower and a peak.[3]
—WILLIAM L. STIDGER

STORY OF THE ARTIST AND THE STATUE:

Auguste Rodin was born in Paris about the middle of the nineteenth century, at a time when there was a lull in art, but he raised statuary art in his country to a higher standard of perfection than it had ever reached in the past. He considered the ancient Greeks masters in sculpture. No one ever executed sculpture as they did; they knew how to make the blood flow in the veins of their statues. As he studied Grecian works of art, he came to the conclusion that their grandeur was due to the expression which the artists were able to put into their figures. There was a repose and restfulness about them which suggested power and strength. This, he believed, came from a constant study of nature.

Rodin said, "Nature is the supreme architect; she makes no mistakes. The sculptor who ignores the teaching offered in the composition of trees, flowers, and crystals falls into the grossest error. He seeks variety and fails to realize that endless diversity can be found in nature." Rodin observed nature in her myriad moods, indulged in walks in field and forest; he studied his models, not as they posed, but in their free, spontaneous movements. Afterwards he worked into his figures the visions thus gained in communion with nature, as did the ancient Greeks.

Rodin built into his own life the beauty and harmony which he saw in nature. His greatness is reflected in some of his writings, among which are the following: "People rush in their enjoyments as well as their business nowadays. I prefer the more tranquil mode. . . . A thing can be beautiful if it is true; outside of truth there is no beauty. Truth itself is nothing more than complete harmony. . . . There is an influence in art which tends to draw men and nations together. . . . As for the future I look forward to it without fear. There is much in nature which suggests fuller beauty in the life beyond."

Rodin believed that the extent of his vision determined the degree of his progress. He saw life clearly and represented it worthily. His sincerity of purpose and truthfulness brought to his art a quality which will make for its survival. In the opinion of many critics, he is the

THE HAND OF GOD, by Auguste Rodin

Moses, **by** Michelangelo

greatest of all French sculptors. He worked with his statues until they seemed to quiver with feeling, and then left them, sometimes with rough lines and unpolished surfaces. By means of the contrast of rough unfinished surfaces with the finished parts, he conveyed his ideas with unusual strength and vividness.

One of his finest creations, which stands unique and apart, is "The Hand of God." With all the science of an anatomist and the art of a sculptor he fashioned an immense hand, strong and smooth. By having the hand disappear beyond the wrist in a huge block of rough, unfinished marble, the sculptor conveys this thought, "No man hath seen God at any time." We see only the work of his hand—beyond that we cannot go. Within the grasp of the hand are two miniature figures, a man and a woman, who have arisen out of the clay from which they were formed. These fragile, pathetic figures represent our first parents. The role of each is indicated—the woman is embracing, while the man is protecting.

Two ideas which the sculptor would convey are: the mystery of creation and divine protection. Here is shown the creative work of God, though it is veiled in mystery. The statue itself is a symbol of life—the two creatures have accepted life with all of its privileges and responsibilities. At the same time they are conscious of their dependence upon the Creator, out of the hollow of whose hand they have just emerged. By placing them safe in the hand of God, the artist is saying that God is sufficient for their every need.[4]

POEM:

>Let me go out to the fields with God,
>And learn from the lily or learn from the sod.
>Let no man speak of a soulless soil
>That gives back the harvest to hands that toil.
>The furrow is laid, and the seed lies there
>Awaiting the sunshine, shower, and air;
>Then the wonder of life leaps up from the grave,
>As the yeoman garners more than he gave.
>The seasons come, and the seasons go,
>And the planters reap as the planters sow;
>Half comes from the seed and half from the sod,
>And all of it comes from the hand of God.

SCULPTURE

Let me go down to the sea with Him,
And follow the tides to the ocean's rim;
Men set their helms for the northern gales,
Or drift where the south winds fill their sails:
They drive till the billows roll white in the dawn;
They drive till the sunset's last splendor is gone.
A thousand fathoms the sea lies deep,
Ten thousand leagues its shore-lines sweep.
But however distant the surgeful shore,
Where lonely isles echo the breakers' roar,—
No matter how far runs our measuring rod,
The mighty sea lies in the hand of God.

Let me look up at the stars with God,
Seeing wonders and glories with mystery shod.
Let me trace the far flight of the comet's dim trail
Past Immensity's gates through Infinity's veil.
Lo, past dreamless voids and staggering heights
Where cherubim wings droop in wearisome flights—
Where the Milky Way drapes, with its white mists sublime,
The womb of creation that gives birth to time—
I follow where spiraling wonders unfold,
And Eternity's outposts stand burnished with gold.
Whether there in the heavens, the sea, or the clod,
The universe lies in the hand of God.[5]

—Robert E. Goodrich

Prayer:

O God, our Father, Creator and Preserver of our lives, we would
enter into communion with thee. Lead us into a greater awareness
of the many ways in which thou art trying to reveal thyself through
the works of thy hand. Forgive us for the times when we have closed
our eyes to thy beauty and our hearts to thy message. As we seek re-
freshment through nature in the out-of-doors, grant us thy peace. May
truth and love possess us completely, driving from us all selfishness,
fear, doubt, or sin. Help us to realize that the force which holds the
universe in place and directs the stars in their courses will also guide
us in our lives. Our Father, we would place our lives in thy hand;

reveal thy will concerning us, and give us courage to follow thy leading.
Through Jesus Christ. AMEN.

HYMN: "From All That Dwell Below the Skies."

BENEDICTION:

May thy peace remain with us as we strive to learn from nature
the secret of harmonious living. AMEN.

SERVICE 15

MOSES

(Michelangelo)

AIM: To help the group to have the right attitude toward God's laws and a greater desire to live by them.

PRELUDE: Hymn tune "Hyfrydol."

CALL TO WORSHIP:

O Lord of life, to thee we lift
Our hearts in praise for those,
Thy prophets, who have shown thy gift
Of grace that ever grows,
Of truth that spreads from shore to shore,
Of wisdom's widening ray,
Of light that shineth more and more
Unto thy perfect day.

Shine forth, O Light, that we may see,
With hearts all unafraid,
The meaning and the mystery
Of things that thou hast made:
Shine forth, and let the darkling past
Beneath thy beam grow bright;
Shine forth, and touch the future vast
With thine untroubled light.

—WASHINGTON GLADDEN

HYMN: "Life of Ages, Richly Poured," or
"Now Thank We All Our God."

MOSES

RESPONSIVE READING:

Leader: Thou, O Lord, shalt endure for ever, and thy remembrance unto all generations. Of old hast thou laid the foundation of the earth; and the heavens are the work of thy hands.

Group: They shall perish, but thou shalt endure; yea all of them shall wax old like a garment; as a vesture shalt thou change them, and they shall be changed: but thou art the same, and thy years shall have no end.

Leader: The children of thy servants shall continue, and their seed shall be established before thee.

Group: Lord, thou hast been our dwelling-place in all generations. Before the mountains were brought forth, or ever thou hadst formed the earth and the world, even from everlasting to everlasting, thou art God.

Leader: For a thousand years in thy sight are but as yesterday when it is past, and as a watch in the night.

Group: We spend our years as a tale that is told.

Leader: So teach us to number our days, that we may apply our hearts unto wisdom.

Group: And establish thou the work of our hands upon us; yea, the work of our hands establish thou it.[1]

UNISON PRAYER OF ADORATION:

Holy, Holy! Lord God Almighty; There is none like unto thee, who hast set thy glory above the heavens. Praise waiteth for thee in Zion, and unto thee shall the vow be performed. Let the words of our mouths and the meditations of our hearts be acceptable in thy sight, O Lord our Strength and our Redeemer. AMEN.[2]

HYMN: "Praise, My Soul, the King of Heaven," or
"O Worship the King."

SCRIPTURE:

And the Lord said unto Moses, Go, get thee down; for thy people, which thou broughtest out of the land of Egypt, have corrupted themselves. They have made them a molten calf, and have worshiped it. And Moses turned and went down from the mount; and as soon as he came nigh unto the camp, he saw the calf: and Moses' anger waxed hot, and he cast the tables out of his hands, and brake them beneath the mount.[3]

STORY OF THE ARTIST AND THE STATUE:

Among the great artists of the Renaissance, Michelangelo Buonarroti stands out, a giant among giants. He was a man of such tremendous power that in one lifetime he accomplished the tasks of a score of men. He excelled in the fields of poetry, painting, sculpture, architecture, and even engineering; but always he thought of himself as a sculptor.

During his early years he showed a skill in sculpture very much like that of the ancient Greeks. He carved a "Cupid" which was buried in the garden to be "accidentally" discovered by some workmen. When found the statue was declared by the authorities of that day to be a genuine antique, the work of one of the Greek masters. But Michelangelo came forward to claim his work, much to the dismay of the authorities.

If Michelangelo had produced no other work of art, his "Moses" would have made him famous, for in this figure is to be seen the perfection of the classic sculptors. As we study this work of art we come to the conclusion that he must have lavished upon it all the skill of his workmanship, coming back to it again and again. But it is singular that his greatest work belongs to an unfinished subject. "Moses" was planned for the tomb of Pope Julius II, as was also the "Bound Slaves." The tomb, however, was never finished and now the statues are separated.

We see in this work of art the grandeur and majesty corresponding with the account of the incident given in the Bible. From the scriptural account we learn that Moses has just returned from Mt. Sinai where he received the Commandments from God. He is shocked to learn that in his absence the Israelites have constructed an idol, a golden calf, to which they are bowing down and worshiping. He is disturbed because they have yielded to the temptation to worship an image, according to the custom of their pagan neighbors.

In this statue, the character of the Israelitish race is plainly written upon the features of Moses. He is seated upon a throne-like chair. His penetrating eyes look into the future to that time when the descendants of Israel shall be as numerous as the sands of the sea. Has not God promised to make of them a great nation? However, there are certain things which God expects of the people. He has given the Commandments which are to be graven upon the hearts of the people instead of upon the tablets of stone. As Moses is ready at the command of God to lead the people into the land which God has promised, they fail to keep their part of the agreement. They have broken the first and greatest of the Commandments by worshiping the golden calf. Moses is disturbed as he thinks of the consequences of this act.

Examine the figure of Moses—the strained twisting of the body, the head raised to the left, one arm thrust forward—all tell of a terrible conflict going on within the man. Here is the expression of a sublime passion. Tense and indignant, he finds it difficult to restrain himself longer. He is not a mere man in a rage—but a prophet who has received his authority from God. He is a leader, entrusted with an important task, but twarted because of the willfulness of his people.

We feel that Moses is restraining himself only until he receives instruction from God. We listen for the moment when he will give vent to his pent-up emotion. We expect to hear the ominous thunder of his voice as he delivers God's message, announcing the dire punishment which must follow the breaking of the Commandment: "Thou shalt not make unto thee any graven image, or any likeness of any thing that is in heaven above, or that is in the earth beneath, or that is in the water under the earth: thou shalt not bow down thyself to them, nor serve them." [4]

POEM:

Each soul must seek some Sinai, as Moses sought of old,
And find immortal music writ on slabs of living gold.
Each soul must seek some Sinai, some high flung mountain peak
Where he may hear the thunders roll and timeless voices speak.
Each soul must seek some Sinai, some secret place apart,
Where he may be alone with God and New-Born Kingdoms chart.
Each soul must seek some Sinai, where God's own voice is heard
And he may see the mystic sign and hear the secret word. [5]
                                        —WILLIAM L. STIDGER

HYMN: "March On, O Soul, with Strength."

POEM:

We know the paths wherein our feet should press,
    Across our hearts are written thy decrees:
Yet now, O Lord, be merciful to bless
    With more than these.

Grant us the will to fashion as we feel,
    Grant us the strength to labor as we know,
Grant us the purpose, ribbed and edged with steel,
    To strike the blow.

Knowledge we ask not—knowledge Thou hast lent,
    But Lord, the will—there lies our bitter need,
Give us to build above the deep intent
    The deed, the deed.[6]

—JOHN DRINKWATER

PRAYER:

Our heavenly Father, we thank thee for the record of the great leaders of the past who have lived according to thy commandments. Grant that as we meditate upon the life of Moses, the great law-giver, we may come to realize the importance of living according to the best we know. Help us in setting up our standards to have an attitude of respect toward law and a greater desire to live by what we believe to be right. Grant that we may demand the best of ourselves and build up an inner discipline which will help us to resist temptation. Forbid that we should ever disappoint our friends who are looking to us as guide or leader. May our courage never falter as we strive to live according to the high standard which we have set for ourselves. For Jesus' sake. AMEN.

BENEDICTION:

Deal gently with us, our Father, and lead us into the paths of righteousness for thy Name's sake. AMEN.

SERVICE 16

FRANCIS ASBURY

(*H. A. Lukeman*)

AIM: Through meditation upon the life of Asbury to lead to a desire to co-operate with the purposes of God.

PRELUDE: "Evening Song" by Schumann.

CALL TO WORSHIP:

> Thee would I sing: thy truth is still the light
> Which guides the nations groping on their way,
> Stumbling and falling in disastrous night,
> Yet hoping ever for the perfect day.
>
> Yes, thou art still the life; thou art the Way
> The holiest know—Light, Life, and Way of heaven;
> And they who dearest hope and deepest pray
> Toil by the truth, life, way that thou hast given.
> —THEODORE PARKER

HYMN: "Just as I Am, Young, Strong, and Free," or "Breathe on Me, Breath of God."

UNISON SCRIPTURE READING:

Blessed is the man that walketh not in the counsel of the ungodly, nor standeth in the way of sinners, nor sitteth in the seat of the scornful. But his delight is in the law of the Lord; and in his law doth he meditate day and night.

And he shall be like a tree planted by the rivers of water, that bringeth forth his fruit in his season; his leaf also shall not wither; and whatsoever he doeth shall prosper.

The ungodly are not so; but are like the chaff which the wind driveth away. Therefore the ungodly shall not stand in the judgment, nor sinners in the congregation of the righteous.

For the Lord knoweth the way of the righteous; but the way of the ungodly shall perish.[1]

PRAYER:

> Take thou our minds, dear Lord, we humbly pray;
> Give us the mind of Christ each passing day;
> Teach us to know the truth that sets us free;
> Grant us in all our thoughts to honor thee.
>
> Take thou our hearts, O Christ, they are thine own;
> Come thou within our souls and claim thy throne;
> Help us to shed abroad thy deathless love;
> Use us to make the earth like heaven above.
>
> Take thou our wills, Most High! hold thou full sway;
> Have in our inmost souls thy perfect way;
> Guard thou each sacred hour from selfish ease;
> Guide thou our ordered lives as thou dost please.
>
> Take thou ourselves, O Lord, heart, mind, and will;
> Through our surrendered souls thy plans fulfill.
> We yield ourselves to thee—time, talents, all;
> We hear, and henceforth heed, thy sovereign call. AMEN.
> —WILLIAM H. FOULKES

POEM:

> I fain would be a sculptor of the soul,
> Making each strong line fine,
>   Each feature faultless.
>   Yet the sculptor cannot carve
>   In wood or stone
>   An image nobler than he sees
>   Within his own stout soul.
>
> So, gazing at the tools within my hand,
> I shudder! How escape from self—
>   Pitiable, limited—

FRANCIS ASBURY

That I may be indeed
God's carver?

Happy is this thought;
There is a Guide for me,
Who in his living flesh
Has given me the perfect image that I seek, of God! [2]
—Toyohiko Kagawa

Hymn:

Great Master, touch us with thy skilful hands;
  Let not the music that is in us die:
Great Sculptor, hew and polish us, nor let,
  Hidden and lost, thy form within us lie.

Spare not the stroke; do with us what thou wilt;
  Let there be naught unfinished, broken, marred;
Complete thy purpose that we may become
  Thy perfect image—thou our God and Lord. [3]
—Horatius Bonar

Story:

During the latter part of the eighteenth century Francis Asbury, the son of a gardener, left his home in West Bronwich, England, to come to America as a missionary. In the years that followed this peasant lad had much to do with molding the life of the new nation. What was the secret of his life? What happened to change him into the leader that he became?

As a lad Francis had a hunger for the things of God. Arising at five o'clock, he walked three miles each morning to attend a prayer service. At eighteen years of age he began preaching. There was little opportunity at that time for a farm lad to secure an education, but his hunger for knowledge was such that he taught himself Latin, Greek, and Hebrew in order better to understand the Bible. As a youth he felt the call to preach the gospel in a land which he had never seen. The sense of a divine mission rested upon him long before he received the appointment to America.

Asbury's entire life was one of self-denial. Coming to America at the age of twenty-six, he never returned to England or saw his parents again. For the sake of the gospel he gave up home and native land and became a homeless wanderer. He traveled incessantly on horseback or in a jolting carriage and endured the hardship of sleeping in the open or in a crowded pioneer cabin. All this he cheerfully endured that the message of the gospel might be taken to the farthest frontier.

It seems that certain men are selected to assume leadership in crucial times. Washington was raised up as a political leader, and Asbury's contribution as a moral and spiritual leader was no less providential. Asbury came to America at a time when the new continent was an uncharted wilderness with only a thin line of population along the Eastern coast. He organized and led a great spiritual movement which affected the entire life of the new nation. Without the work of Christian ministers such as he, the nation would have had a less secure foundation.

Although much credit is due to those who worked with him, his singleness of purpose, his vision of the future, his patience under trying circumstances, made him the peer among them all. With exacting ideals and a zeal which drove him to incessant labor, he set a pace which was too strenuous for most people of his day. For example, at the close of the year when he moved from his first circuit, the services of eight men were required to carry on his work.

During the Revolutionary period, when most of the English ministers returned to the mother country, Asbury decided to remain in America regardless of the danger to his own life. At the close of the conflict, when new territory was being settled, ministers were needed in the new communities. It was Asbury's custom to visit each of these places before assigning a minister. Although he served the whole of America, the circuit was made frequently, from New England to Georgia, and from the Atlantic Coast to the most remote western frontier. He traveled more than six thousand miles on horseback each year in all kinds of weather and averaged a sermon a day for forty-five years. When past seventy years of age and broken in health, he continued to travel, even though he had to be lifted on his horse.

Asbury's wise judgment, his knowledge of men, and his life-long devotion to the cause of Christ made him an ideal leader. The fact that he did not seek for himself a course easier than that of the most humble man in the ranks had a great effect upon the men with whom he labored. They could not afford to be less sacrificing, less heroic than their leader. The result was that a whole generation of workers was transformed into heroic ministers who set themselves to the task of evangelizing an entire continent. Asbury's contribution to America is recognized in the erection of a statue to his honor in the national capital.

On the occasion of a visit to Washington a minister while looking at this equestrian statue of Asbury remarked, "I do not like that horse. He looks so tired. Asbury always rode a good horse." His companion replied, "But you must not lose sight of the fact that Asbury wore out a number of horses traveling as he did. No doubt his horse was tired most of the time."

POEM:

> It is easy to foot the trodden path
>   Where thousands walked before,
> It is simple to push my fragile bark
>   Past the reefs of a charted shore.
>
> I find it good to ride the road
>   Where others laid the rail.
> It is well to test the ocean's strength
>   Where others also sail.
>
> But when a dream enslaves a man,
>   A dream of the vast untrod,
> A dream that says, "Strike out with me,
>   Strike out or part with God,"
>
> A dream that leads to an untried path
>   Where unknown tempests blow,
> And the only chart a man can boast
>   Is the will that bids him go,
>
> Ah, then, my soul, bethink yourself,
>   For God has spread this scroll
> To test the stuff of your rough-hewn faith
>   And the fiber of your soul.[4]
>   —PERCY R. HAYWARD

PRAYER:

O God of all nations, we thank thee for our native land, for the privileges and opportunities which we share. We thank thee for the great leaders of the past who have brought our nation to its place of leadership. We thank thee for the ministers of all denominations, and we are grateful for the heritage which they have passed on to us. We thank thee that thou hast dignified life by calling us to be co-laborers with thee. Help us to be faithful to the trust committed to us. Teach us to love our country and be loyal to its ideals. Grant that no word, thought, or act of ours may ever endanger the freedom for which our forefathers labored so valiantly. For Jesus' sake. AMEN.

HYMN: "Forward Through the Ages," or
"My Country, 'Tis of Thee," or
"Are Ye Able?"

BENEDICTION:

The grace of our Lord Jesus Christ, the love of God, and the communion of the Holy Spirit, be with you all. AMEN.

SERVICE 17

MARGARET OF NEW ORLEANS

(*Alexander Doyle*)

AIM: To help the group to realize the value of a life that is completely dedicated to Christian service.

PRELUDE: "Ave Maria" by Schubert.

CALL TO WORSHIP:

> As the sun doth daily rise,
>   Brightening all the morning skies,
> So to thee with one accord
>   Lift we up our hearts, O Lord!
>
> Be our guard in sin and strife;
>   Be the leader of our life;
> Lest from thee we stray abroad,
>   Stay our wayward feet, O Lord!
>
> Quickened by the Spirit's grace
>   All thy holy will to trace,
> While we daily search thy word,
>   Wisdom true impart, O Lord!
>   —ANONYMOUS

HYMN: "We Thank Thee Thy Paths of Service Lead," or "Work for the Night Is Coming."

CONFESSION OF FAITH:

I believe in God, who is for me spirit, love, the creator of all things.

I believe that God is in me, as I am in him.

I believe that the true mission of man is in living the will of God.

I believe that in living the will of God there can follow nothing except good for me and for others.

I believe that the will of God is that we should love our fellowmen, and do unto others as we would have them do unto us.

I believe that the reason of life is for each of us to grow in love.

I believe that this growth in love will help to bring the Kingdom of God on earth.

I believe that the will of God has never been more clearly expressed than in the teachings of Jesus.

I believe that this teaching will be for the good of all, will save mankind, and give this world the greatest happiness.[1]

UNISON PRAYER:

> Like the lightning, make me fearless,
>   Like the moonlight, gentle, kind,
> Like the mountain, strong and patient,
>   Like thyself, by love refined.
>
> Like the water, make me useful,
>   Like the stars, to live by plan,
> Like the winds, forever active,
>   Like thyself, in loving man. AMEN.[2]
>   —CHAUNCEY R. PIETY

SCRIPTURE:

I beseech you therefore, brethren, by the mercies of God, that ye present your bodies a living sacrifice, holy, acceptable unto God, which is your reasonable service. And be not conformed to this world: but be ye transformed by the renewing of your mind, that ye may prove what is that good, and acceptable, and perfect will of God.[3]

POEM:

> Slowly, by thy hand unfurled,
> Down around the weary world
> Falls the darkness, O, how still
> Is the working of thy will.

MARGARET OF NEW ORLEANS

Mighty Maker, ever nigh,
Work in me as silently;
Veil the day's distracting sights,
Show me heaven's eternal lights.

Living worlds to view he brought
In the boundless realms of thought;
High and infinite desires,
Flaming like those upper fires.

Holy truth, eternal right,
Let them break upon my sight,
Let them shine, serene and still,
And with light my being fill.
—WILLIAM H. FURNESS

STORY:

Simple goodness and practical charity were the feminine virtues immortalized in the first statue erected to a woman in the United States. In the beautiful old city of New Orleans there lived a humble heroine whose name today is more widely honored than that of any other in the city.

Margaret Haughery, born in the city of Baltimore in the year 1815, was left an orphan when but a child. Her parents, immigrants from Ireland, had come to this country with a great hope for the future, but shortly after their arrival were stricken with yellow fever. Margaret was taken into a home where she received splendid care but no formal education.

Marrying in her early teens, Margaret moved to New Orleans, where she had the misfortune to lose her husband and her only child. Her own experience as an orphan caused her to seek relief from her sorrow through helping orphans as much as her limited means permitted. Being unable to read or write, she found few lines of work open to her. For a time she was employed as a laundress in one of the hotels of the city, and out of her meager earnings a portion was saved for the orphans.

Margaret's real opportunity came when she entered the domestic service of the Poydras Orphan Asylum. Toiling early and late, at all sorts of work, from scrubbing to dairying, she found happiness in the service she was able to render to the poor. Later she went out collecting food and money. Her plain rough features and her simple costume became familiar in the markets, shops, and stores all over the city. For ten years she labored in this Home. When a new building was needed Margaret and one of the Sisters of Charity raised the entire sum—a great undertaking for two women in those days. Next she built a home for infants and also a home for older girls where they could learn trades and fit themselves for employment.

Margaret's next business venture was to open up a small dairy with her own savings. The small milk cart, driven by the plain-faced woman, became a familiar sight on the streets of New Orleans. Sometimes a stranger would ask, "Who is that woman?" And the answer invariably was, "That is Margaret, the Orphans' Friend." The people almost forgot that she had any other name. Despite the fact that she could neither read nor write, Margaret had business judgment to the extent that her counsel was sought by successful businessmen. Through a loan to a baker who had failed in business, she came into possession of a bakery. This afforded her another opportunity of helping the poor. In spite of enormous quantities of bread that she gave away, her business developed and eventually became the largest bakery in the city.

Although her income had doubled many times, Margaret did not change her manner of living. She went about as before selling milk and making bread deliveries with her little cart. She dressed in the plain skirt and loose sacque which were a familiar costume from one end of New Orleans to the other. Upon being asked why she did not wear better clothes, she replied, "How can I when there is so much suffering in the world?" Appeals for help were always answered regardless of race or creed. She forgot herself completely in her desire to help unfortunate people.

The three largest homes for children in New Orleans are almost entirely the result of Margaret's efforts, while the home for the aged and infirm is also one of her benefactions. For forty-six years she toiled for others and accumulated over a million dollars, all of which was expended on the poor. Without education, with no capital except common sense, integrity, and a desire to help, she accomplished a great work. In her last illness the wealthiest and most fashionable ladies of the city considered it a privilege to minister to her needs. When she died, on February 9, 1882, bankers, merchants, city officials, and people from all walks of life gathered at her funeral. On the next Sunday the subject used in practically all the pulpits was the story of Margaret's life.

Two years later the city of New Orleans erected a statue to Margaret's honor on the site which she had saved as a playground for the orphans. Although the city had ordered a fire station to be erected on this location, she implored the city fathers to donate the ground to the children, and it was done. The statue stands on Camp Street in front of the orphanage where she began her work as a domestic servant. It represents her sitting in a rustic chair, clothed in the familiar skirt and sacque, with an arm encircling a small child. The word "Margaret" is carved on the pedestal. The strong, kindly face looks down with serenity upon the children who crowd about the statue to spell out the name cut in the marble, and to hear the story of the woman who gave her life for motherless children. At the unveiling of the monument it was said of her: "The substance of her life was charity; the spirit of it, truth; the strength of it, religion; the end, peace—then fame and immortality."

PRAYER:

O Lord, who though thou wast rich, yet for our sakes didst become poor, and hast promised in thy gospel that whatsoever is done unto the least of thy brethren, thou wilt receive as done unto thee; give us grace, we humbly beseech thee, to be ever willing and ready to minister, as we are able, to the necessities of our fellow-creatures, and to extend the blessings of thy kingdom over all the world, to thy praise and glory forever. AMEN.[4]

HYMN: "O Master, Let Me Walk with Thee."

BENEDICTION:

Keep us as thine own, O God, and fill our hearts with love for the poor. Through Jesus Christ our Lord. AMEN.

ABRAHAM LINCOLN

(Augustus Saint-Gaudens)

AIM: To lead the group to a keener appreciation of the truths which Abraham Lincoln exemplified in his life.

PRELUDE: Hymn tune "Via Militaris."

CALL TO WORSHIP:

> Gather us in, thou Love that fillest all;
>   Gather our rival faiths within thy fold;
> Rend each man's temple veil, and bid it fall,
>   That we may know that thou hast been of old.
>
> Gather us in; we worship only thee;
>   In varied names we stretch a common hand;
> In diverse forms a common soul we see;
>   In many ships we seek one spirit-land.
>
> Some seek a Father in the heavens above;
>   Some ask a human image to adore;
> Some crave a spirit vast as life and love;
>   Within thy mansions we have all and more.
>   —GEORGE MATHESON

HYMN: "God of the Nations, Near and Far," or "God of the Strong, God of the Weak."

PRAYER:

Eternal God, our Maker and our Lord, Giver of all grace, from whom every good prayer cometh, and who poureth thy spirit upon all who seek thee; deliver us, when we draw nigh to thee, from coldness of heart and wanderings of mind; that with steadfast thoughts and pure affections we may worship Thee in spirit and in truth through Jesus Christ our Lord. AMEN.[1]

UNISON READING:

> Now praise we great and famous men,
>   The fathers, named in story;
> And praise the Lord, who now as then
>   Reveals in man his glory.
>
> Praise we the wise and brave and strong
>   Who graced their generation;
> Who helped the right, and fought the wrong,
>   And made our folk a nation.
>
> Praise we the great of heart and mind,
>   The singers sweetly gifted,
> Whose music like a mighty wind
>   The souls of men uplifted.
>
> Praise we the peaceful men of skill,
>   Who builded homes of beauty,
> And, rich in art, made richer still
>   The brotherhood of duty.
>
> Praise we the glorious names we know,
>   And they whose names are perished—
> Lost in the haze of long ago—
>   In silent love be cherished.
>
> In peace their sacred ashes rest,
>   Fulfilled their day's endeavor;
> They blessed the earth, and they are blessed
>   Of God and man, for ever.[2]
>   —WILLIAM GEORGE TARRANT

RESPONSIVE READING:

Leader: Fourscore and seven years ago our fathers brought forth on this continent a new nation, conceived in liberty, and dedicated to the proposition that all men are created equal.

Group: We hold these truths to be self evident: that all men are created equal; that they are endowed by their Creator with certain inalienable rights; that among these are life, liberty, and the pursuit of happiness;

Leader: That to secure these rights, governments are instituted among men, deriving their just powers from the consent of the governed.

Group: With malice toward none, with charity for all, with firmness in the right as God gives us to see the right.

Leader: To bind up the nation's wounds; to care for him who shall have borne the battle, and for his widow and orphan—to do all which may achieve and cherish a just and lasting peace among ourselves and with all nations.

Group: In the name of God we lift our banner, and dedicate it to peace, union, and liberty, now and forevermore.[3]

POEM:

Not in vain the distance beacons—forward, forward let us range,
Let the great world spin forever down the ringing grooves of change;
Through the shadow of the globe we sweep ahead to heights sublime,
We, the heirs of all the ages in the foremost files of time.

O, we see the crescent promise of man's spirit has not set;
Ancient founts of inspiration well through all his fancy yet;
And we doubt not through the ages one increasing purpose runs,
And the thoughts of men are widened with the process of the suns.

Yea, we dip into the future, far as human eye can see,
See the vision of the world, and all the wonder that shall be,
Hear the war drum throb no longer, see the battle flags all furled,
In the Parliament of man, the Federation of the world.

—ALFRED TENNYSON

INTERPRETATION:

The "Abraham Lincoln" of Saint-Gaudens has been acclaimed by critics the greatest work of art of its type in the United States. There can be no doubt that the sculptor has produced a masterpiece. Sculpture by its inflexible nature limits the expression to the enduring and monumental. Lincoln, with his qualities of grandeur, stability, and integrity, is a suitable subject for sculpture. These qualities, along with the simplicity and ruggedness of the man, have been seized, and the sculptor has given this homely figure a power of appeal which is irresistible.

The sculptor's idea was a novel one, that of introducing a chair from which Lincoln has arisen and is about to speak. He is looking down at an imaginary audience with an expression of seriousness which is almost sad. The pose is easy and natural; standing with bowed head, he seems to be lost in thought. The statue is planted firmly on the right foot, while the right hand behind the back gives balance to the figure. The left foot is advanced and the left hand grasps the lapel of the coat in a gesture that is usually associated with a man of action.

The chair is essential, but as we come under the spell of the commanding figure of Lincoln it seems to disappear. The bowed head suggests sympathy and tenderness; the broad shoulders bespeak his strength. To combine tenderness and strength in a work of art is not an easy matter, but Saint-Gaudens has accomplished that difficult task. As we study the statue, all other details are lost to sight, and the expression of the face holds our attention. The sculptor has shown his genius in taking a rugged, gnarled figure and giving it grace and charm. He has revealed the romance and poetry of Lincoln, along with his rugged manhood. In fact, he has portrayed a type of man which we most admire and revere.

The statue calls to our mind a few of the characteristics of Lincoln. As a lad he learned from his mother a firm belief in God and in the ultimate triumph of the right. It has been difficult for some to understand why Lincoln, holding such ideas, did not unite with the Church. During his latter years he wrote these lines which will shed some light: "When any Church will inscribe over the altar, as its sole qualification for membership, the Master's condensed statement of both the law and the gospel, 'Thou shalt love the Lord thy God with all thy heart, soul, mind, and strength, and thy neighbor as thyself'; that Church will I join."

When the fate of the nation hung in the balance, Lincoln formulated many of his policies during periods of prayer. As he walked under the trees in the quiet of the night, the decision must have come to him that "this nation under God shall have a new birth of freedom." On one occasion he prayed, "Teach me, O God, to know thy will. Teach me to read thy difficult purpose, here, which must be plain if I had eyes to see it. Make me just." He determined that the war must be conducted on a national basis, transcending all party lines. He said, "In great contests each party claims to act in accordance with the will of God. Both may be and one must be wrong. One cannot be for and against the same thing at the same time. In the present Civil War it is possible that God's purpose is something quite different from the purpose of either party."

Lloyd George said in speaking of Lincoln, "I doubt whether any statesman who ever lived sank so deeply into the hearts of the people of many lands as Abraham Lincoln did. I am not sure that you in America realize the extent to which he is also our possession and our pride. His courage, fortitude, patience, humanity, and clemency, his trust in the people, his belief in democracy, and, may I add, some of the phrases in which he gave expression to the attributes, will stand out forever as beacons to quiet troubled nations and their perplexed leaders. Resolute in war, he was moderate in victory. Misrepresented, misunderstood, underestimated, he was patient to the last. But the people believed in him all the time, and they still believe in him.

"In his life he was a great American. He is an American no longer. He is one of those giant figures, of whom there are few in history, who lost their nationality in death. They are no longer Greek, Hebrew, English, or American—they belong to mankind. . . . Abraham Lincoln belongs to the common people of every land."

POEM:

> We need him now—his rugged faith that held
>   Fast to the rock of Truth through all the days
> Of moil and strife, the sleepless night; upheld
>   By very God was he—that God who stays
> All hero-souls who will but trust in him,
>   And trusting, labor as if God were not.
> His eyes beheld the stars, clouds could not dim
>   Their glory; but his task was not forgot:
> To keep his people one; to hold them true
>   To that fair dream their fathers willed to them—
> Freedom for all; to spur them; to renew
>   Their hopes in bitter days; strife to condemn.

ABRAHAM LINCOLN

Such was his task, and well his work was done—
Who willed us greater tasks, when set his sun.[4]
                                        —Thomas Curtis Clark

Directed Meditation:

As we think of the life of this great man, let us meditate upon the ideals for which he stood: liberty, justice, the worth of human personality, and the rights which should be accorded to each individual. As a nation are we cherishing these ideals? What are some of our national sins? Are we in any way personally responsible for the sins of our nation? Is our love of country based upon the highest type of patriotism? Are we living in such a way that we may have peace among ourselves and with other nations? As we wait in silence before God, let us ask him to reveal to us our personal responsibility for upholding the ideals of our nation. . . . Amen.

Poem:

Is there no fighting
　　Now to be done?
Joy in brave conflict,
　　Victories won?
Is there, because we bid
　　Carnage to cease,
No splendid warfare,
　　Conquests of peace?

You of the keen eye,
　　Hand quick and sure,
Clear mind and body
　　Trained to endure—
You of the high heart,
　　Scornful of greed,
Thrilling to beauty,
　　Pain and stark need.

Trumpets are sounding!
　　Spring to the call,
Hold high your banner
　　Never to fall!

Fight! for the conquest
  Of hatred and fear,
Dare to push onward,
  O young pioneer!

"He that overcometh
  Shall have a new name. . . ."
Not in the warfare
  Of poison and flame,
Storm the far ramparts
  Of wisdom's increase,
Free the last captive,
  Good soldiers of peace! [5]
          —EDITH KENT BATTLE

HYMN: "God of Our Fathers, Whose Almighty Hand," or
  "Faith of Our Fathers."

BENEDICTION:

Lord of the nations, thus to thee
  Our country we commend;
Be thou her refuge and her trust,
  Her everlasting Friend. AMEN.
          —JOHN R. WREFORD

SERVICE 19

THE PIONEER MOTHER

(*Alexander Proctor*)

AIM: To help the group to appreciate the heritage which has come to them from the pioneers.

PRELUDE: Hymn tune "Materna."

CALL TO WORSHIP:

O God, thou art my God; early will I seek thee: my soul thirsteth for thee, my flesh longeth for thee in a dry and thirsty land where no water is. As the hart panteth after the water brooks, so panteth my soul after thee, O God. My soul thirsteth for God, for the living God. Deep calleth unto deep at the noise of thy waterspouts.

HYMN: "O Beautiful for Spacious Skies," or
  "Faith of Our Fathers."

UNISON SCRIPTURE READING:

Now faith is the substance of things hoped for, the evidence of things not seen. For by it the elders obtained a good report. Through faith we understand that the worlds were framed by the word of God, so that things which are seen were not made of things which do appear. By faith Abraham, when he was called to go out into a place which he should after receive for an inheritance, obeyed; and he went out, not knowing whither he went. By faith he sojourned in the land of promise, as in a strange country, dwelling in tabernacles with Isaac and Jacob, the heirs with him of the same promise: for he looked for a city which hath foundations, whose builder and maker is God. These all died in faith, not having received the promises, but having seen them afar off, and were persuaded of them, and embraced them, and confessed that they were strangers and pilgrims on the earth. For they that say such things declare plainly that they seek a country. And truly, if they had been mindful of that country from whence they came out, they might have had opportunity to have returned. But now they desire a better country, that is, an heavenly: wherefore God is not ashamed to be called their God: for he hath prepared for them a city.[1]

THE LORD'S PRAYER.

OFFERING.

OFFERTORY PRAYER:

> All things are thine; no gift have we
> Lord of all gifts, to offer thee:
> And hence with grateful hearts today
> Thine own before thy feet we lay.
>
> Thy will was in the builders' thought;
> Thy hand unseen amidst us wrought;
> Through mortal motive, scheme, and plan,
> Thy wise, eternal purpose ran.
>
> In weakness and in want we call
> On thee for whom the heavens are small;
> Thy glory is thy children's good,
> Thy joy, thy tender fatherhood. AMEN.
> —JOHN GREENLEAF WHITTIER

POEM:

> O you youths, Western youths,
> So impatient, full of action, full of manly pride and friendship,
> Plain I see you Western youths, see you tramping with the foremost,
> Pioneers! O pioneers!
>
> All the past we leave behind,
> We debouch upon a newer mightier world, varied world,
> Fresh and strong the world we seize, world of labor and the march,
> Pioneers! O pioneers!

THE PIONEER MOTHER

We primeval forest felling,
We the rivers stemming, vexing we and piercing deep the mines within,
We the surface broad surveying, and the virgin soil upheaving,
    Pioneers! O pioneers!

O you daughters of the West!
O you young and elder daughters! O you mothers and you wives!
Never must you be divided, in our ranks you move united,
    Pioneers! O pioneers!

Has the night descended?
Was the road of late so toilsome, did we stop discouraged nodding on
        our way?
Yet a passing hour I yield you in your tracks to pause oblivious,
    Pioneers! O pioneers!

Till with sound of trumpet,
Far, far off the daybreak call—hark! how loud and clear I hear it wind,
Swift to the head of the army!—swift! spring to your places,
    Pioneers! O pioneers! [2]

—WALT WHITMAN

INTERPRETATION OF THE STATUE:

"The Pioneer Mother," a bronze group, stands in Penn Valley
Park in Kansas City, Missouri. This statue, composed of a group of
figures, shows the Pioneer Mother on horseback, holding an infant,
her face set toward her future home; at her right is her young husband
leading a horse, and on the other side is the guide. The group is so
arranged that the woman is the central figure. This group immor-
talizing the pioneer mother has had much favorable criticism from art
critics. It is considered one of the finest statues of pioneer life in
America.

This work of art was presented to Kansas City by the late Howard
S. Vanderslice in honor of his mother, who made the journey from
Kentucky to White Cloud, Kansas, about the middle of the nineteenth
century. On the stone pedestal supporting the figures are carved the
words of Ruth, which are appropriate as a scriptural text for such a
journey: "Whither thou goest, I will go; and where thou lodgest, I
will lodge: thy people shall be my people, and thy God my God."

SCULPTURE

Alexander Proctor, the artist who designed the memorial, is a Canadian whose parents were pioneers. While living in Denver, Colorado, he demonstrated his skill as an artist by sketching the wild animals he encountered on his hikes. For weeks at a time he would lose himself wandering about the peaks of the Rockies studying and sketching animals. Later he studied in New York and in Paris, where many honors came to him. His work may be seen in the Metropolitan, Corcoran, and other Museums of Art, and his statues are in parks and zoological gardens across the country from New York to Denver. Among his prized pieces, "The Pioneer Mother" is the most impressive and depicts truthfully the spirit of those heroic adventurers who settled this country of ours.

The artist has shown the hardy pioneers setting out with a resolute will to push back the horizon. Enjoying the benefits of civilization as we do today, we find it difficult to visualize the hardship and suffering which they were called upon to bear. What led the pioneer woman and her husband to leave familiar scenes and journey to the far west? Was it a spirit of restlessness or a desire for adventure that caused them to follow an ever-advancing frontier? There was a vision which lured them on—a vision of the opportunities awaiting them in the unsettled country.

The pioneers made their way over unmarked trails and through dense wilderness, scaled mountain peaks, and at the end of the journey built their cabins on the edge of the clearing. Making a home and wresting a living from an unwieldy soil required courage and hardihood. Such problems as famine, drought, dust-storms, and contending with warlike Indians tested the very fiber of the soul. But they faced it all with an unconquerable spirit and eventually carved a home out of a vast wilderness.

Through it all the pioneer woman stood beside her husband, bearing her share of hardship without complaint. She did not mind the privations, physical suffering, or the sacrifice. At first the solitude and the vastness of the country may have overwhelmed her, but hardest of all to bear was having her children grow up without the advantages of an education. Self-sacrifice is a small thing as compared to this. Ofttimes her thoughts were of friends and relatives left behind, but her love for her husband outweighed it all and gave her courage to make the venture.

Mrs. Aldrich in her novel *A Lantern in Her Hand* tells an interesting story of pioneer life and closes with the following picture of the mother: "Abbie sat looking out at the family gathered there in the beautiful sun-parlor, sat there with half-closed eyes like an old Buddha looking out on the generations. Eighty years of living were behind her, most of them spent in fighting—fighting the droughts, the snows, the hot winds, the prairie fires, the blizzards, fighting for the children's physical, mental, and spiritual development, fighting to make a civilization on the raw prairie. Bending her back to the toil, hiding her heart's disappointments, giving her all in service, she was like an old mother partridge who had plucked all the feathers from her breast for the nest of the young." [3]

Poem:

> Bright—bright the flickering hearth-fire's gleam!
> But he heard the call of a restless dream:
> > "Get you out, and away!
> Turn your back on hearth and kin,
> There's new land for the brave to win—
> Over the crest of the misty hills,
> A bridgeless river its wild flood spills;
> Unhewn forests and sunburnt plains
> Call to freedom, and richer gains,
> > Out on the untried way!"
> How bright—how warm the hearth-fire's gleam!
> She saw in his eye the brighter dream.
>
> Slowly, beyond the wilderness' rim,
> He broke the trail, and she followed him
> > All the way, to a home!
> In covered wagon, or jolting cart,
> She held the hearth-fire's glow, in her heart;
> Facing danger, conquering fear,
> Keeping his hopes and visions clear,
> Teaching the children remembered ways,
> Learning new skills, through lonely days,
> > Looking ahead, to a home!
> His vision led over the wilderness' rim—
> She guarded the hearth-fire's glow, for him. [4]
>
> > —Edith Kent Battle

PRAYER:

We thank thee for the heritage which has come to us from the pioneers who have pushed their way through the wilderness to settle this vast country of ours. We thank thee for those who have toiled for us and made our lot easier. We realize that others have blazed the way and that we are now entering into their labors. We thank thee for the high idealism—the principles of freedom, justice, and truth—upon which our country was founded. May we guard this truth and pass it on untarnished to future generations. We thank thee for the record left of the home life of the pioneers—their love and loyalty to each other. Grant that in building our homes we may build on as firm a foundation as did they. For Jesus' sake. AMEN.

HYMN: "America Triumphant! Brave Land of Pioneers," or
    "The Land We Love Is Calling."

BENEDICTION:

The grace of our Lord Jesus Christ, the love of God, and the communion of the Holy Spirit, be with you all. AMEN.

ABRAHAM LINCOLN, by Augustus Saint-Gaudens

The Pioneer Mother, by Alexander Proctor

The Scout, by Cyrus Edwin Dallin

SERVICE 20

THE SCOUT

(*Cyrus Edwin Dallin*)

AIM: To help the group to appreciate the spirit which leads one to sacrifice self for others.

PRELUDE: "By the Waters of Minnetonka" by Thurlow Lieurance.

CALL TO WORSHIP:

Come ye, and let us walk in the light of the Lord. He will teach us of his ways, and we will walk in his paths.

Lighten our darkness, we beseech thee, O God. Reveal thyself unto us as we worship thee.

HYMN: "Go, Labor On," or
        "O God Our Help in Ages Past."

UNISON READING: "A Psalm in Indian Sign Language."

The Great Father, above, a Shepherd Chief is. I am his, and with him I want not. He throws out to me a rope, and the name of that rope is love, and he draws me, and he draws me, and he draws me to where the grass is green and the water not dangerous, and I eat and drink and lie down satisfied.

Sometimes my heart is very weak and falls down, but he lifts it up again, and draws me into a good road.

His name is wonderful.

Sometime, it may be very soon, it may be longer, it may be a long, long time, he will draw me into a place between mountains.

It is dark there, but I'll draw back not. I'll be afraid not, for it is there between those mountains that the Shepherd Chief will meet me,

and the hunger I have felt in my heart all through this life will b
satisfied.

Sometimes he makes the love rope into a whip, but afterwards h
gives me a staff to lean on.

He spreads a table before me with all kinds of food, and we si
down and eat that which satisfies us. He puts his hand upon my hea
and all the "tired" is gone.

My cup he fills till it runs over.

What I tell you is true, I lie not.

These roads that are "away ahead" will stay with me through thi
life, and afterwards I will go to live in the Big Tepee and sit down wit
the Shepherd Chief forever.[1]

PRAYER OF A NAVAJO INDIAN:

> Lord of the mountain,
> Hear a young man's prayer.
> Hear a prayer for cleanness.
> Keeper of the strong rain
> Drumming on the mountain,
> Lord of the small rain
> That restores the earth in newness,
> Keeper of the clean rain,
> Hear a prayer for wholeness.
> Keeper of the paths of men,
> Hear a prayer for straightness,
> Hear a prayer for courage.
> Lord of the thin peak,
> Keeper of the headlands,
> Keeper of the strong rocks,
> Hear a prayer for staunchness,
> O, Lord, and spirit of the mountain.
> —AUTHOR UNKNOWN

SCRIPTURE:

As the Father hath loved me, so have I loved you: continue ye
my love. If ye keep my commandments, ye shall abide in my lov
even as I have kept my Father's commandments, and abide in h
love. These things have I spoken unto you, that my joy might r
main in you, and that your joy might be full. This is my comman

ᴴᵉⁿᵗ, That ye love one another, as I have loved you. Greater love ath no man than this, that a man lay down his life for his friends.[2]

ᴛᴏʀʏ ᴏꜰ Tꜱᴀʟɪ, ᴛʜᴇ Cʜᴇʀᴏᴋᴇᴇ:

Word had gone out that gold had been discovered in the Cherokee ands between the Chestatee and the Smokies. The Cherokees, a roud and powerful nation, once held a vast domain, but now occu-ied an area about the size of the present state of Massachusetts. By treaty the Government had guaranteed this territory to them for-ver; but, after the discovery of gold, a new treaty was forced upon them by which they agreed to give up their homeland and be deported the west on the condition that they be paid $5,000,000. Their chief, ohn Ross, voiced their protest against so great an injustice, since nly about one-sixth of the tribe had been consulted. But the white an had decided that the Indians must go. Not only was there gold the mountains, but there were rich farms in the coves and valleys.

Tsali, working on his farm, began to hear rumors that the sol-iers were building stockades into which the Indians were being erded until they could be deported to the west. He went about his ork as one in a dream. He was thinking, not so much of his own xile, but of the homeland. His people had lived here from the be-inning. They had hunted in the mountains, and tilled their crops the valley of the Ocona Luftee. And now it seemed that no one ould be left to carry on the traditions of the people or to guard the acred places. Surely there must be a way.

In the spring of 1838, the soldiers began pouring in until there ere seven thousand of them. Taking away the Indians' rifles, they erded them into pens where they were held until they could be de-orted. When the soldiers came for Tsali he seemed to be in a daze. Ie paid little attention to the fact that they already had his brother, is two grown sons and their families as prisoners. As one in a dream e motioned to his wife and younger son to follow, and together they arted the steep climb to the nearest stockade.

Although old, Tsali was strong and vigorous; his wife seemed lder and was unable to travel fast. A soldier prodded her with his ayonet in order to quicken her pace. At her cry of pain, the lethargy ropped from Tsali, and he sprang like a panther upon the soldier, king his weapon from him. At the same moment the other Indians ttacked. When the struggle was over one soldier was dead and the

others had fled. Tsali and his party escaped into the wildest part o
the mountains near Clingman's Dome, where they were joined late
by a few who managed to escape from the stockades.

During the summer four thousand Cherokees were deported b
steamers down the Tennessee River, thence to the Mississippi, and o
to the Indian Territory. So many died on the way that Chief John Ros
asked that the remainder be allowed to make the trip overland unde
their own chiefs. Wagons were provided for the small children, th
aged, and the sick, while the rest of the group made the journey o
foot. Each day there were deaths—sometimes as many as twent
Their noted chief Whitepath and the wife of John Ross died on th
way. For many of them it was a March of Death—for all of them
Trail of Tears. Six months passed before the tragic journeyed ende
and one-fourth of their number had died on the way, either of sic
ness or exposure.

Tsali and his party, hidden away safely in the most inaccessibl
part of Clingman's Dome, were spared this harrowing experienc
They had lived in peace, for the soldiers had been occupied wit
guarding and removing the seventeen thousand refugees. But no
the General turned his attention to the fugitives who had escape
With his seven thousand soldiers loosed to find the fugitives, their fa
was inevitable. Yet to find their hiding place was not easy. It prom
ised to be a bloody fight, since the Indians had sworn that they woul
not leave the mountains. The General decided to send a message t
Tsali, giving him an opportunity to surrender. A white trader, Wi
liam Thomas, in whom the Indians had confidence, was delegated t
carry the message to Tsali, promising him that if those who had she
blood—he, his brother, and his sons—would give themselves up, th
rest of the party would be allowed to remain at peace in the homelan

The white man found his way to Tsali's cave by secret trails an
was invited to sit in the circle around the campfire. The Indiar
listened gravely to the proposition of the General. Tsali sat lookin
over the valley below and to the mountains beyond. This beautifu
country—their homeland—was theirs no longer. He thought of th
pathetic army of his people marching into exile. The little grou
about him had looked to him to find a way to remain in the hom
land. They might be the nucleus for a new nation that would carr
on the customs and guard the sacred places. He looked at his broth
and his sons as they waited for him to speak. Tsali's face was o

and haggard, but a new light came into his eyes as he answered, "We will come."

Tsali knew what he was doing; he knew exactly what to expect. They could face the firing squad, for they were dying for their people, that the remnant might remain in the ancient homeland. He, his brother, and his three sons went in and gave themselves up. The General spared the younger son because of his youth. The others were taken to a spot near the mouth of Ocona Luftee, just outside the boundary of what is now the Great Smoky Mountains National Park. A squad of Cherokee prisoners was compelled to fire the fatal shots.

Tsali's eyes as he faced the firing squad were the eyes of a conqueror. No doubt he was looking into the future to the time when a new nation would be born. This country would again be the home of his people. Perhaps he saw hundreds of Indian cabins with children playing about them, the men hunting deer in the mountains while the women went about their work. The ancient ways were being carried on while his people grew and waxed strong in the shadow of the Great Smokies.

Tsali and his kinsmen did not die in vain. The little band of fugitives has grown until it now numbers over thirty-two hundred. Although they have taken on the white man's ways and learned his language, they still carry on their ancient customs and guard the sacred places in the reservation provided for them by the Government in the shadow of the Great Smokies. It may be that in the future a fitting memorial will be erected to Tsali and his kinsmen on the point of Clingman's Dome.

POEM:

> Christ Jesus knew no foreigner,
>   Nor any foreign strand;
> He loved his neighbors, one and all,
>   Of every tribe and land.
>
> Christ Jesus knew no color line,
>   And no inferior race;
> He'd make the world a brotherhood,
>   And live in every face.[3]
>
> —CHAUNCEY R. PIETY

Prayer:

O God, the Father of us all, thou who didst manifest thy love by sending thy Son into the world, grant unto us a new insight into the meaning of his life. As thy love was perfected in Christ, help us to understand the meaning of thy commandment to love one another. As we think of the beauty of Christ's sacrificial life, grant that we may be willing to sacrifice for others, loving one another in word and in deed. As we meditate on the sacrifice of these brothers of ours in giving their lives for their kinsmen, help us to appreciate their efforts to guard their sacred places and preserve their ancient customs. Help us to have a brotherly attitude toward persons of all races and forbid that we should ever be a stumbling block to any of them in their upward climb. Through Jesus Christ. Amen.

Hymn: "O Brother Man, Fold to Thy Heart."

Benediction:

The Lord bless you, and keep you;
The Lord make his face shine upon you, and be gracious unto you;
The Lord lift up his countenance upon you, and give you peace.
Amen.

SERVICE 21

CHRIST OF THE ANDES

Aim: To lead to the conviction that God the Father of all would have the nations live together in love and in co-operation with each other.

Prelude: "Kamennoi-Ostrow" by A. Rubenstein.

Call to Worship:

God be merciful unto us, and bless us; and cause his face to shine upon us: that thy way may be known upon earth, thy saving health among all nations.

Let the people praise thee, O God; let all the people praise thee.

O let the nations be glad, and sing for joy; for thou shalt judge the people righteously and govern the nations upon earth.

Let the people praise thee, O God; let all the people praise thee. Then shall the earth yield her increase; and God, even our own God, shall bless us. God shall bless us; and all the ends of the earth shall fear him.[1]

Hymn:

> O God, beneath thy guiding hand
> Our exiled fathers crossed the sea;
> And when they trod the wintry strand,
> With prayer and psalm they worshiped thee.

> Thou heard'st, well pleased, the song, the prayer:
> Thy blessing came; and still its power
> Shall onward, through all ages, bear
> The memory of that holy hour.

Laws, freedom, truth, and faith in God
    Came with those exiles o'er the waves;
And when their pilgrim feet have trod,
    The God they trusted guards their graves.

And here thy Name, O God of love,
    Their children's children shall adore,
Till these eternal hills remove,
    And spring adorns the earth no more.[2]
                    —LEONARD BACON

UNISON SCRIPTURE READING:

But in the last days it shall come to pass, that the mountain of the house of the Lord shall be established in the top of the mountains, and it shall be exalted above the hills; and the people shall flow to it. And many nations shall come, and say, Come, and let us go up to the mountain of the Lord, and to the house of the God of Jacob; and he will teach us of his ways, and we will walk in his paths.

I will make with them a covenant of peace. Thus shall they know that I the Lord their God am with them, and that they are my people, saith the Lord God.

Arise, shine; for thy light is come, and the glory of the Lord is risen upon thee. For, behold, the darkness shall cover the earth, and gross darkness the people: but the Lord shall arise upon thee, and his glory shall be seen upon thee. And the Gentiles shall come to thy light, and the kings to the brightness of thy rising.

Therefore thy gates shall be open continually; they shall not be shut day nor night; that men may bring unto thee the forces of the Gentiles, and that their kings may be brought. For the nation and kingdom that will not serve thee shall perish; yea, those nations shall be utterly wasted. I will also make thy officers peace, and thine exactors righteousness. Violence shall no more be heard in thy land, wasting nor destruction within thy borders; but thou shalt call thy walls Salvation, and thy gates Praise.[3]

PRAYER.

        God of the nations, hear our call;
        Thou who art Father of us all,
        Show us our part in thy great plan
        For the vast brotherhood of man.

In plastic form the nations lie;
For molding unto us they cry;
May we their urgent summons heed
And gladly go to meet their need.

May we, a nation blessed with light,
Be ever truer to the right,
That nations in our life may see
The power which we derive from thee.

Let us with earnestness of youth
Care only for pursuit of truth.
O may we feel thy guidance still
And heed the impulse of thy will.

Thus, as thy Kingdom cometh here,
Shall it throughout the world draw near;
And loyalty to country then
Shall reach out to include all men. Amen.
　　　　　　　　　—Vera Campbell

Story:

For many years there had been a dispute over the boundary line between two South American countries. Each nation claimed territory the other was unwilling to grant, and each thought that its demand in the argument was just. The borderline between Argentina and Chile lies at the summit of a very high mountain in the Andes where the land is so rugged that it is of little value. Nevertheless, statesmen lost their tempers, the people became aroused, and there was talk of war. Both countries began preparing to fight, men were called upon to enlist, and the manufacture of ammunition was hastened.

Bishop Benavente of Argentina was distressed about the preparation for war. It seemed to him a mistake to take up arms against their neighbors who had done no wrong. Surely there must be another way for Christians to settle the dispute. At any rate he would bring the matter to the attention of his congregation. On Easter Sunday, when the church was filled with people, the Bishop closed his message with the remark, "We seem to have forgotten the commandment of Jesus to love one another. It would be a crime for us to go to war with Chile over so trifling a matter. Let us take our dispute to someone outside of both countries, submit the matter to arbitration, and thus save the lives of our young men."

The Bishop wondered whether the people would receive his suggestion favorably. The news of the sermon spread through both countries. When it reached Bishop Java on the other side of the mountain, he reacted in the same manner concerning war. He said, "Why should Christians fight each other? Let us settle this matter in a peaceable manner." So he went from town to town preaching against it. Finally the two nations agreed to cease their preparation for war and allow a disinterested person to settle their dispute. King Edward VII of England was selected to arbitrate the matter, and the war was never waged.

The men whom King Edward sent to examine the boundary line discovered that each country was right about some of the land, but wrong about other parts. A correct line was drawn which was satisfactory to both nations, and there was great rejoicing that a happy solution of the difficulty had been reached. Both countries further agreed that hereafter all of their disputes should be settled by arbitration, which seemed to be a better method than fighting.

Bishop Benavente had often expressed the desire that at some time the figure of Christ should stand on the summit of one of the mountains. It seemed that now was the logical time to erect a statue in honor of Christ, the Prince of Peace. An Argentine woman, Senora de Costa, suggested, "We have no need now for our weapons of war. Let us take all the guns and cannon which have been bought to kill one another and melt them and mold a great statue of Christ. Then let us place it on top of the highest mountain between the two countries, where it will stand as a monument of peace forever." The women, in order to show their gratitude for the peaceable settlement of the difficulty, went to work to raise money with which to buy the cannon. In a short while a bronze figure of Christ was constructed which was more than twice life-size.

The statue was taken high above the timber line, to a jagged crest at the summit of a pass in the Andes. It was brought by rail part of the way and was hauled by mules the remainder of the distance. Here it stands today in the perpetual snow on the boundary line between the two countries. Mounted on a stone pedestal of rough-hewn natural rock, the figure of Christ is poised upon a globe, holding a cross in one hand; the other is raised aloft as though he were speaking to the people on both sides of the mountain urging them to love one another. On a square medallion below the statue are two figures embracing each other and holding a scroll on which an inscription is written.

On the evening before the unveiling of the statue, many of the leaders of both countries were encamped near the borderline on top of the mountain. Early the next morning thousands of people gathered for the celebration, and their cheers and singing could be heard far into the valleys. As the people gazed upon the face of Christ, they thanked God that war had been averted and pledged themselves always to keep peace. Reverently the Bishop read the inscription on the base of the monument:

> "Sooner shall these mountains crumble into dust than Argentina and Chile shall violate the peace they have pledged at the feet of Christ the Saviour."

Now for more than four decades peace and good will have prevailed between these two countries.

POEM:

Over all earth's troubled nations, shadowed by clouds of war,
Shines a hope bedimmed yet glorious, white and tranquil as a
      star—
Hope that will not fade in darkness, though fulfilment may seem
      far—
      The day of peace will come!

Though now spite and mad ambition blind the rulers of the State,
Though the crafty politicians their unhallowed schemes debate,
Man at last shall know the folly of relentless greed and hate—
      The day of peace will come!

Lawless dreams of selfish empire for a time may daze and lure;
Only truth will stand forever, only justice will endure;
Right and brotherhood may tarry, but their victory is sure—
      The day of peace will come!

— 139 —

O true hearts of every nation, in these dark, tumultuous years,
Never cease to pray and labor, never yield to coward fears!
Men shall yet beat swords to plowshares and to pruning hooks
  their spears—
      God's promised peace will come! [4]
                —EFFIE SMITH ELY

PRAYER:

O God, our Father, thou who hast made of one blood all nations, grant that all people may be united in one holy bond of truth and peace, of faith and love; may we put away anything which would hinder us from living together as thy children. In all our relations may we show love, justice, and consideration for other nations. Grant that there may be a growing desire for brotherhood among nations, a willingness to seek the welfare of all. Forgive the narrowness which causes us to think only of ourselves. Forgive all of our national sins, and grant that we may live in love and brotherhood with all people everywhere. Help us to remember that the greatness of a nation consists not in the abundance of material possessions, but in unselfish service rendered. Inspire the leaders of the nations with a breadth of vision, and may thy spirit so rule their hearts that justice and peace may prevail everywhere. Guide those who take counsel for the nations, give unto them insight and wisdom that good will, justice, and peace may come to all nations; through Jesus Christ, the Prince of Peace. AMEN.

HYMN: "Come! Peace of God," or
      "In Christ There Is No East or West."

BENEDICTION:

May the Spirit of Christ abide with you, leading you in the ways of peace. AMEN.

PART THREE

HYMNS

SERVICE 22

O LOVE THAT WILT NOT LET ME GO

(*George Matheson*)

AIM: To lead the individual facing insecurity to realize that there is a
power in the Christian religion which will undergird his life
and help him to live victoriously in the midst of difficult situations.

PRELUDE: Hymn tune "Consolation" (Mendelssohn).

CALL TO WORSHIP:

> Father of lights, in whom there is no shadow,
>   Giver of every good and perfect gift!
> With one accord we seek thy holy presence,
>   Gladly our hearts to thee in praise we lift.
>
> Light of the world, through whom we know the Father!
>   Pour out upon us thine abiding love,
> That we may know its depth and height and splendor,
>   That heaven may come to earth from heaven above.[1]
>   —ELIZABETH WILSON and HELEN THOBURN

HYMN: "Love Thyself Last," or
       "Saviour, Thy Dying Love."

RESPONSIVE READING:

Leader: God is love; and he that dwelleth in love, dwelleth in God,
       and God in him.

Group: Strong Son of God, immortal Love,
       Whom we, that have not seen thy face,

By faith, and faith alone, embrace,
Believing where we cannot prove;

Leader: Commit thy way unto the Lord, trust also in him, and he shall bring it to pass.

Group: Thou seemest human and divine,
　　　The highest, holiest manhood, thou:
　　　Our wills are ours, we know not how;
Our wills are ours, to make them thine.

Leader: In all thy ways acknowledge him, and he shall direct thy paths.

Group: Our little systems have their day;
　　　They have their day and cease to be;
　　　They are but broken lights of thee,
And thou, O Lord, art more than they.[2]

PRAYER:

O Lord of love, in whom we live and move and have our being, kindle in our souls thy fire of love. May we be so rooted and grounded in love that we can understand the meaning of thy love which sent Christ into the world to show us the way of life. Grant that our lives may not be restricted by selfishness. Give us the grace to be true helpers of all we contact; and may our sympathy extend not only to those by whom we are bound by tender ties of love, but may it reach all people. Let nothing come between us to cloud our trust of each other. Suffer us not to darken thy world by thoughts of resentment or revenge, but give us the power to bring in the reign of love among men. In Jesus' name. AMEN.

POEM:

　　　Time is itself a restless dream:
　　　A swallow's flight across a stream;
　　　Life's dawn and twilight come so soon
　　　The dusk of evening nudges noon;
　　　A flash, a flame, a flickering;
　　　The flutter of a weary wing;
　　　A pitcher broken at the well:
　　　A whispered word, a muffled bell:

O LOVE THAT WILT NOT LET ME GO

But Ah! the gods are good to me:
Love lives through all Eternity! [3]
—WILLIAM L. STIDGER

STORY OF THE AUTHOR AND THE HYMN:

George Matheson as a youth was blessed with health, wealth, and natural talents which fitted him for the ministry, his chosen profession. But at the age of fifteen he was stricken with a disease which affected the nerves of his eyes and caused him to lose his sight. A weaker person would have given up in discouragement, but he went ahead resolutely and was graduated from the University of Glasgow at nineteen years of age. Soon afterwards he entered the ministry of the Church of Scotland.

In spite of his handicap, Dr. Matheson became one of the ablest ministers of his day. His first parish was Innellan, on the Firth of Clyde, where he remained for eighteen years. In addition to his labors as a minister, he was able to do a vast amount of literary work. Of his twenty-five published volumes, many were the most widely read of that day. His preaching attracted such attention that he was summoned to preach before Queen Victoria. Delighted with his sermon, the queen presented him with a small bust of herself instead of the customary signed photograph which was usually given to her friends.

At the age of forty-four Dr. Matheson was called to St. Bernard's in Edinburgh, where he rose to the height of his power and influence. The immense crowds attending his services marveled at the way he would take his verses in the responsive readings, announce several hymns, and go through the entire service without an error. There was something about his messages which went straight to the hearts of his listeners. His prayers were such that the worshipers felt that they were in the presence of God. Through his gracious personality he won the hearts of all who knew him, and many were encouraged and uplifted by the courageous spirit with which he faced the affliction in his life.

Concerning the inspiration of the hymn, Dr. Matheson said: "My hymn was composed in the manse at Innellan on the evening of June 6, 1882. I was at that time alone. It was the day of my sister's marriage, and the rest of the family were staying overnight in Glasgow. Something had happened to me which was known only to myself, and which caused me the most severe mental suffering. This hymn was the fruit of that suffering. It was the quickest bit of work I ever did in my life. I had the impression of having it dictated to me by some inward voice rather than working it out myself. I am quite sure it never received at my hands any retouching or correction. The writing of this hymn was a unique experience. All of my other poems are manufactured articles, but this hymn came like a day-spring from on high. I have never been able to gain once more the same fervor in verse." [4]

We can only conjecture as to the experience which caused him such severe mental suffering. Some say that it was because blindness was coming upon him, but that affliction had come at least twenty years prior to this time. Others say that his fiancee rejected him because of approaching blindness. The facts in the case do not bear out either story. Instead of being the sentimental suffering of a rejected lover, this hymn is the autobiography of one who lived a radiant Christian life, full of confidence and hope. Dr. Matheson was able to bear his affliction, for God was to him "the Love that never failed and the Light that followed all the way." Naturally one who lived a triumphant life would not brood over sorrow, but instead would give his life back to God in renewed surrender.

Dr. Matheson's life is a challenge to those who are living on the ragged edge of insecurity, suffering from frustration, inner conflicts, and fears. He shows a way out for those who are trying to bear burdens in their own strength. He appropriated a power beyond himself, which came from God. Instead of worrying about circumstances over which he had no control, he submitted himself to the will of God, put himself in harmony with God's great purpose, and thereby found his larger self. The religion of Christ furnished the undergirding of his life, bore him up and carried him over the hard places, and helped him to live creatively and abundantly.

The theme of this hymn is self-renunciation. In the first stanza the author speaks of surrendering his life, giving it back to God in order that he may come into possession of the richer, fuller life. In the second stanza he speaks of his own light as a flickering torch which is borrowed from another source, but which by dedicating it to God becomes brighter and fairer. In the third stanza he contrasts joy with pain and recalls the fact that the rainbow can be seen only through the rain. Forgetting the sorrows of the present moment, he looks forward to that morning that shall tearless be. Tennyson expressed a similar thought in the following lines:

"I held it truth, with him who sings
    To one clear harp with divers tones,
    That men may rise on stepping-stones
Of their dead selves to higher things."

In the last stanza, Dr. Matheson gives the solution which he found, that of putting his own selfish ambitions in the background and surrendering his will to God. He says: "I remember having seen a gardener bend down a blood-red flower and cover the seed of it with the earth, leaving it there throughout the winter months. Next spring the seed sprang up and burst forth in blood-red blooms. So, the thought came to me, 'If I lay down as in dust all my ambitions, all I am seeking for myself, and give my life to God in full surrender, I shall know what it is to possess and live the full, rich life—the life that shall never end.'"

HYMN:

O Love that wilt not let me go,
    I rest my weary soul in thee;
I give thee back the life I owe,
That in thine ocean depths its flow
    May richer, fuller be.

O Light that followest all my way,
    I yield my flickering torch to thee;
My heart restores its borrowed ray,
That in thy sunshine's blaze its day
    May brighter, fairer be.

O Joy that seekest me through pain,
    I cannot close my heart to thee;
I trace the rainbow through the rain,
And feel the promise is not vain
    That morn shall tearless be.

O Cross that liftest up my head,
    I dare not ask to fly from thee;

I lay in dust life's glory dead,
And from the ground there blossoms red
  Life that shall endless be.
                    —GEORGE MATHESON

POEM:

We sigh for human love, from which
  A whim or chance shall sever,
And leave unsought the love of God,
  Though God's love lasts forever.

We seek earth's peace in things that pass
  Like foam upon the river,
While, steadfast as the stars on high,
  God's peace abides forever.

Man's help, for which we yearn, gives way,
  As trees in storm-winds quiver,
But, mightier than all human need,
  God's help remains forever.

Turn unto thee our wavering hearts,
  O thou who failest never;
Give us thy love and thy great peace,
  And be our help forever! [5]
                    —EFFIE SMITH ELY

PRAYER:

Our Father, thou who art worthy of a love greater than we can give or understand, make thy presence known unto us. Thou who art more ready to hear than we are to pray, harken unto our supplication. Create within us a desire to follow thy leading and to live according to thy purpose for us. Make us vessels fit to be used of thee. Grant that nothing may seem too hard to do or to suffer in obedience to thee. Grant that we may not so much seek to be loved as to love, to be understood as to understand, to be served as to serve; for it is in giving that we receive, it is in pardoning that we are pardoned, and it is in dying to ourselves that we become new creatures in Christ Jesus our Lord. AMEN.[6]

BENEDICTION:

May the peace and love of God abide with you forever. AMEN.

SERVICE 23

DEAR LORD AND FATHER OF MANKIND

(John Greenleaf Whittier)

AIM: To lead the group into a new insight of the value of waiting
quietly before God, thus allowing him to reveal himself through
silent meditation.

PRELUDE: "Quietude" by Louis Gregh (Opus 53).

CALL TO WORSHIP:

> Come, O thou God of grace,
> Dwell in this holy place,
>   E'en now descend!
> This temple, reared to thee,
> O may it ever be
> Filled with thy majesty,
>   Till time shall end!
>
> Be in each song of praise
> Which here thy people raise
>   With hearts aflame!
> Let every anthem rise
> Like incense to the skies,
> A joyful sacrifice,
>   To thy blest name!
>   —WILLIAM E. EVANS

HYMN: "Still, Still with Thee," or
"Lord, Speak to Me, that I May Speak."

HYMNS

UNISON SCRIPTURE READING:

I will lift up mine eyes unto the hills, from whence cometh my help.

My help cometh from the Lord, which made heaven and earth.

He will not suffer thy foot to be moved: he that keepeth thee will not slumber.

Behold, he that keepeth Israel shall neither slumber nor sleep.

The Lord is thy keeper; the Lord is thy shade upon thy right hand.

The sun shall not smite thee by day, nor the moon by night.

The Lord shall preserve thee from all evil: he shall preserve thy soul.

The Lord shall preserve thy going out and thy coming in from this time forth, and even for evermore.

He that dwelleth in the secret place of the Most High shall abide under the shadow of the Almighty.

My soul, wait thou only upon God; for my expectation is from him.[1]

PRAYER:

O God, our Father, teach us to be still and know that thou art God. Grant unto us a sense of thy presence. Take away from us any thought or selfish desire that would shut thee out. Give unto us a revelation of thyself which will enable us to live according to thy purpose for us in the world. Incline our hearts to keep thy commandments, and guide our feet into the paths of righteousness, for Jesus sake. AMEN.

POEM:

Dear God of Life, the Truth, the Way,
    The Changeless Purpose thou;
Vouchsafe thy spirit that it may
    Reveal thy nearness now.

Thy providence, like shifting stars,
    Shines on the darkened hour,
And in the night the mystic bars
    Of music sing thy power.

The lonely shepherd on the moor
   Lifts up his heart to thee,
And in the wonder of the lure
   He knows security.

The strength of eagles winging higher,
   Is naught compared with thine;
And broken songs in martyr fires
   Have made that strength divine.

So, Lord, dear hope of all our ways,
   And calm of our despair,
Make strong our lives and glad our days
   Through love's unwearying prayer.
         —WILLIAM E. DUDLEY

STORY OF THE AUTHOR AND THE HYMN: [2]

This beautiful prayer hymn, "Dear Lord and Father of Mankind," was written by one of the best-loved American poets, John Greenleaf Whittier. With characteristic modesty the poet once remarked, "I am not really a hymn-writer, for the good reason that I know nothing of music. A good hymn is the best use to which poetry can be devoted, but I do not claim to have succeeded in composing one." Although it is true that only a few of his poems were written for singing, choice passages have been taken from his poems and have been set to music by great composers. More than fifty of his hymns, still in use, are included in modern hymnbooks.

Whittier was born on a farm near the Merrimac River, a few miles from Haverhill, Massachusetts. He gives an attractive picture in his "Snowbound" of the home life on this secluded farm. Working on a farm during the week and attending the Quaker meeting on the Sabbath was his custom. Though he lived in humble surroundings throughout his early years, a knowledge of the outside world came to him from visitors marooned in his home on account of snowbound roads. Books were scarce, but a copy of the *Poems and Songs of Robert Burns* was given to him by one of his teachers. He became so fascinated with the poems that he had a great desire to write with the beauty and simplicity of the Scottish poet. Surely if a plowman could write with such feeling of commonplace things, a farm lad could learn to do the same.

The neighborhood school furnished Whittier his early education. By teaching, binding books, and doing other odd jobs, he worked his way through Haverhill Academy. His career as a writer began when he became editor of a country newspaper. From the beginning his writings appealed to the people, for, having had similar experiences, he understood their problems. Although living in a dreamland of poetry, he kept in close touch with the practical affairs of everyday life.

Whittier was a member of the Society of Friends and used their mode of speech and style of dress throughout his lifetime. From his parents he inherited a deep devotional nature and an independent spirit. In his poems are reflected the strict Quaker teachings and the principles of religion which governed his life. His hymns express a faith in the abiding presence of God and a dependence upon the goodness of God.

In order fully to appreciate the meaning of the hymn, "Dear Lord and Father of Mankind," we must see it in its original setting as a part of the poem "The Brewing of Soma." In this poem Whittier describes the ancient practice of the priests in the old Vedic days of preparing "Soma," the drink of the gods. After drinking the strange concoction, the priests and people worked themselves into a religious frenzy. They went into strange ecstasies of joy until they reached the point of physical exhaustion, and then sobered they sank to the earth. Thinking of this as worship, they imagined the intoxication to be a sacred exultation which showed that they were God-possessed.

Though this happened in the "morning twilight" of the race, the poet realized that they were not the only ones who worked themselves into a frenzy in worship. He accused some of his own day of indulging in similar practices. He pointed out that by means of music, incense, or vigils they tried to bring the skies nearer, or to lift themselves up to heaven. In striking language he portrayed the folly of such attempts, whether practiced in the days when the light was dim, or at a later day. He said,

> And yet the past comes round again,
> And new doth old fulfill;
> In sensual transports wild as vain
> We brew in many a Christian fane
> The heathen Soma still! [3]

DEAR LORD AND FATHER OF MANKIND

Whittier passes on this thought to us: we are guilty of like folly if we work ourselves up into emotional excitement and imagine it to be spiritual ecstasy. In the following lines he points out the value of seeking God in the silence and in the stillness, learning the beauty of his peace.

Dear Lord and Father of mankind,
  Forgive our feverish ways;
Reclothe us in our rightful mind,
In purer lives thy service find,
  In deeper reverence, praise.

In simple trust like theirs who heard,
  Beside the Syrian sea,
The gracious calling of the Lord,
Let us, like them, without a word
  Rise up and follow thee.

O Sabbath rest by Galilee!
  O calm of hills above,
Where Jesus knelt to share with thee
The silence of eternity,
  Interpreted by love!

Drop thy still dews of quietness,
  Till all our strivings cease;
Take from our souls the strain and stress,
And let our ordered lives confess
  The beauty of thy peace.[3]

PRAYER:

Our Father, we thank thee for thine inward voice, which ever and again calleth us away from the clamor and dusty strife of this life into the cool, quiet groves of eternity. We thank thee that close around us, ever pressing in upon our minds is thine eternal world, full of peace and joy. We thank thee that a hundred times a day we may take refuge therein, feel thy cool fingers soothing our fevered foreheads, look steadily into thy quiet eyes, drink in unto our souls from that gaze the strength and peace of eternity.[4] Grant unto us an awareness of thy presence; take from our lives the strain and stress of feverish haste and worry. May we have the assurance that our lives are being lived according to thy will and purpose for us. For Jesus' sake. AMEN.

POEM:

> I will pray when morning glory
>   Gilds the eastern hills with gold,
> When the dew has washed the tulip
>   And dawn's tale of time is told.
> I will kneel before thine altars
>   And burn incense at thy shrines;
> Incense of the rose and lilac,
>   Locust bloom and wind-washed pines.
>
> I will pray at noon, dear Master,
>   When all life is high with hope
> And the sun has halved the circle
>   In its mighty sweep and scope;
> When life's blood is coursing wildly
>   In a full majestic stream,
> When the tide of strength is running
>   To its daring flow and dream.
>
> I will pray, dear God, when darkness
>   Throws its vesper shadows 'round,
> In the silence I will listen,
>   Kneeling on thy holy ground.
> I will meet thy tryst at twilight,
>   When the silent shadows sleep,
> And all the birds and beasts and children
>   Into dreamland softly creep.[5]
>   —WILLIAM L. STIDGER

HYMN: " 'Mid All the Traffic of the Ways," or
     "O for a Closer Walk with God."

BENEDICTION:

May the peace of God which passeth all understanding abide with you forever. AMEN.

SERVICE 24

O GOD, OUR HELP IN AGES PAST

(*Isaac Watts*)

Aim: To lead the group into a greater confidence in the help which comes from God.

Prelude: "Liebestraum" by Franz Liszt.

Call to Worship:

> How lovely is thy dwelling place,
>   O Lord of hosts, to me!
> The tabernacles of thy grace,
>   How pleasant, Lord, they be!
>
> My thirsty soul longs ardently,
>   Yea, faints thy courts to see:
> My very heart and flesh cry out,
>   O living God, for thee.
>
> Behold, the sparrow findeth out
>   An house wherein to rest;
> The swallow also for herself
>   Provided hath a nest;
>
> Even thine own altars, where she safe
>   Her young ones forth may bring,
> O thou Almighty Lord of hosts,
>   Who art my God and King.

Blest are they in thy house that dwell,
    They ever give thee praise.
Blest is the man whose strength thou art,
    In whose heart are thy ways.[1]

HYMN: "Now Thank We All Our God," or
"From All That Dwell below the Skies."

RESPONSIVE READING:

Leader: God is our refuge and strength, a very present help in trouble

Group: Therefore will not we fear, though the earth be removed
and though the mountains be carried into the midst of the
sea;

Leader: Though the waters thereof roar and be troubled, though the
mountains shake with the swelling thereof.

Group: The Lord of hosts is with us; the God of Jacob is our refuge.

Leader: In thee, O Lord, do I put my trust; let me never be ashamed
deliver me in thy righteousness.

Group: Bow down thine ear to me; deliver me speedily: be thou my
strong rock, for an house of defense to save me.

Leader: For thou art my rock and my fortress: therefore, for thy
name's sake, lead me and guide me.

Group: Into thine hand I commit my spirit: thou hast redeemed me,
O Lord God of truth.

Leader: I will be glad and rejoice in thy mercy: for thou hast considered my trouble; thou hast known my soul in adversities.

Group: My times are in thy hand: deliver me from the hand of mine
enemies, and from them that persecute me.

Leader: Make thy face to shine upon thy servant: save me for thy
mercies' sake.

Group: Oh how great is thy goodness, which thou hast laid up for
them that fear thee; which thou hast wrought for them that
trust in thee before the sons of men!

Leader: Thou shalt hide them in the secret of thy presence from the
pride of man; thou shalt keep them secretly in a pavilion
from the strife of tongues.

O GOD, OUR HELP IN AGES PAST

Group: Be of good courage, and he shall strengthen your heart, all ye that hope in the Lord.[2]

PRAYER:

Almighty God, Father of all mercies, we, thine unworthy servants, do give thee most humble and hearty thanks for all thy goodness and loving-kindness to us and to all men. We bless thee for our creation, preservation, and all the blessings of this life; but above all for thine inestimable love in the redemption of the world by our Lord Jesus Christ; for the means of grace, and for the hope of glory. And, we beseech thee, give us that due sense of all thy mercies, that our hearts may be truly thankful, and that we show forth thy praise, not only with our lips, but in our lives, by giving up ourselves to thy service, and by walking before thee in holiness and righteousness all our days, through Jesus Christ our Lord, to whom, with thee and the Holy Ghost, be all honor and glory, world without end. AMEN.[3]

POEM:

> O Love divine, that stooped to share
>   Our sharpest pang, our bitterest tear!
> On thee we cast each earthborn care;
>   We smile at pain while thou art near.
>
> Though long the weary way we tread,
>   And sorrow crown each lingering year,
> No path we shun, no darkness dread,
>   Our hearts still whispering, "Thou art near!"
>
> When drooping pleasure turns to grief,
>   And trembling faith is changed to fear,
> The murmuring wind, the quivering leaf,
>   Shall softly tell us thou art near!
>
> On thee we fling our burdening woe,
>   O Love divine, forever dear!
> Content to suffer while we know,
>   Living and dying, thou art near!
>   —OLIVER WENDELL HOLMES

HYMNS

When Isaac Watts was a youth, he criticized the hymns of his day, until it was suggested, in a bantering way, that he might try to write something better. He said nothing about it, but quietly went to work to supply a need which he was one of the first to see. The metrical versions of the Psalms which were used as hymns were crude and difficult to sing. The Psalms were read a line at a time by a clerk; and the congregation, after singing the line, waited for the next to be read. Watts said, "It happens that the part of the service which should be the highest peak in the worship is in reality the worst. We preach the gospel and pray in Jesus' name, why not have hymns based upon the teachings of Jesus and in the language of our own day?"

It was only natural that there should be opposition, for some of the people were of the opinion that Watts was taking too much liberty with the word of God. He replied, "The Bible is God's word to us and our songs are our word to him. Does it not seem that we have the same right to compose songs as to pray an original prayer?" In spite of severe criticism, he went ahead and in a few years arranged many of the Psalms as well as other scriptural passages in English verse. His next task was to write hymns which expressed religious experience common to his day. This brought additional criticism, but gradually the people began to realize the value in singing hymns which expressed their own experiences.

Watts began writing verse at an early age, and throughout his school days continued the custom. In this way he was unconsciously preparing himself for the career of a hymn writer. His first volume of poems was received favorably, and won for the youthful writer an honorable place among the English poets of his day. Hymnbooks and other literary works followed rapidly until he had published more than fifty volumes. In his day he was a popular pastor, serving an Independent church in London for almost half a century; but he is remembered today because of his hymns, and is known as "the Father of English Hymnody."

When Watts began writing hymns he had no idea that they would be used anywhere except in the humble Independent chapels, but they became so popular that the hymnbooks were literally thumbed out of existence. In all he produced more than six hundred hymns, many of which are the greatest written in any age. His hymns, lofty and majestic, are still used after more than two hundred years by English-speaking people in every country. When Watts died, he was honored by his nation with a memorial in Westminster Abbey. His gift for writing had placed him among other great writers of the world. The artist, in designing the statue, showed Watts seated at a desk writing as an angel bends over him whispering the thoughts which were written into his hymns.

On one occasion, when Watts was reading a portion of the Scripture, the Psalm took such a hold on him that he could not put it out of his mind. Under the inspiration of the moment, he wrote the hymn, "O God, Our Help in Ages Past." As we study the hymn, we find that it is a paraphrase of the ninetieth Psalm, which the Hebrews had used in worship from the earliest times. In singing this hymn we feel a kinship with that countless throng of people who in times of persecution put their trust in God and found him sufficient for all their needs. Let us strive to catch the spirit of the hymn and sing it with understanding. It has changed the entire outlook and attitude toward life of many persons from the most humble to the greatest. It will help us to commit our lives to God with confidence and go forth in the assurance that he will provide strength for every trial.

During the World War, at a time when the outlook was discouraging, a mass of people filled Trafalgar Square in London. The Lord Mayor and many other notables were present. As the people, led by a group of choirs and accompanied by the regimental band, lifted their hearts to God in an outburst of song, Watts' hymn was used. It seemed to those present that the nation was committing itself in trust to God as the mighty concourse of people sang the hymn. Certainly our need of God today is as great as it has ever been in any age.

LITANY OF ADORATION:

Leader: Lord, thou hast been our dwelling place in all generations.

Group: (to be sung)

> O God, our help in ages past,
>   Our hope for years to come,
> Our shelter from the stormy blast,
>   And our eternal home!

Leader: Before the mountains were brought forth, or ever thou hadst formed the earth and the world, even from everlasting to everlasting, thou art God.

Group: Under the shadow of thy throne
    Still may we dwell secure;
Sufficient is thine arm alone,
    And our defense is sure.

Leader: Thou turnest man to destruction; and sayest,
    Return, ye children of men.

Group: Before the hills in order stood,
    Or earth received her frame,
From everlasting thou art God,
    To endless years the same.

Leader: For a thousand years in thy sight are but as yesterday when it is past, and as a watch in the night.

Group: A thousand ages, in thy sight,
    Are like an evening gone;
Short as the watch that ends the night,
    Before the rising sun.

Leader: Thou carriest them away as with a flood; they are as a sleep: in the morning they are like grass which groweth up. In the morning it flourisheth, and groweth up; in the evening it is cut down, and withereth.

Group: O God, our help in ages past,
    Our hope for years to come;
Be thou our guide while life shall last,
    And our eternal home! AMEN.[4]

BENEDICTION:

    Father, give thy benediction,
      Give thy peace before we part;
    Still our minds with truth's conviction;
      Calm with trust each anxious heart.

    Let thy voice with sweet commanding,
      Bid our grief and struggles end;
    Peace which passeth understanding
      On our waiting spirits send. AMEN.
                —SAMUEL LONGFELLOW

SERVICE 25

WHERE CROSS THE CROWDED WAYS OF LIFE

(*Frank Mason North*)

AIM: To lead to a greater awareness of the needs of throngs crowding the cities.

PRELUDE: Hymn tune "Morecambe."

CALL TO WORSHIP:

Sing unto the Lord a new song and his praise from the end of the earth.

Let the wilderness and the cities thereof lift up their voice.

Let the inhabitants of the rock sing, let them shout from the top of the mountains.

Let them give glory unto the Lord, and declare his praise in the islands.

HYMN: "The Light of God Is Falling," or
"Go Labor On, Spend and Be Spent."

INVOCATION:

Spirit of God, whose very Name, the Comforter, maketh melody above the noises and confusions of our life, fulfill thy gentle ministries to these waiting hearts of ours, that with reverent assurance we may take thy Name upon our lips, and speak to thee and one another in the comfortable words of holy song.[1] We are never more conscious of our need than when we approach thee in prayer. Draw near to us until we become aware of a sense of thy presence. Cleanse our thoughts, forgive our foolish ways, and lead us into the way of truth. In Jesus' name. AMEN.

HYMNS

Leader: Bear ye one another's burdens.

Group: We bear the strain of earthly care,
  But bear it not alone;
 Beside us walks our Brother Christ
  And makes our task his own.

Leader: Let us not be weary in well doing: for in due season we shall
reap, if we faint not.

Group: Through din of market, whir of wheels,
  And thrust of driving trade,
 We follow where the master leads,
  Serene and unafraid.

Leader: As we have therefore opportunity, let us do good unto all men.

Group: The common hopes that make us men
  Were his in Galilee:
 The tasks he gives are those he gave
  Beside the restless sea.

Leader: Come unto me, all ye that labor and are heavy laden, and I
will give you rest.

Group: Our brotherhood still rests in him,
  The Brother of us all,
 And o'er the centuries still we hear
  The Master's winsome call.[2]

POEM:

O righteous Father, Source of all in One,
Mirrored for man in thy clear-crystal Son,
 The shadows lift—
That we may see, undimmed, thy perfect gift!

Not merely, long ago, a blessed Child,
Divine Evangel, Prophet undefiled,
 But—now and here—
The ardent Christ who challenges our fear.

Show us again the Christ who walked alone
Yet felt the push of crowds, who made his own

The outcast poor,
All beaten, troubled souls, beset, unsure.

The Christ whose keen, uncompromising glance
Can pierce our armored selves with bright, swift lance
Straight to the heart;
From whose clear presence hate and lust depart.

Open our eyes, that we say see—stark, plain—
Our greed and cowardice, our brother's pain,
His fear, his need,
Close interwoven by our selfish creed.

Father, in whom love must begin and end,
Give us the will, the courage, to defend
That unmost shrine
Where love and sacrifice become divine—

Faith irresistible, to see and dare
Eternity's adventures, made aware
Of undivided Three,
Thyself, thy love in man, and man in thee! [3]
—EDITH KENT BATTLE

SCRIPTURE:

When he saw the multitudes, he was moved with compassion on them, because they fainted, and were scattered abroad as sheep having no shepherd. And when he was come near, he beheld the city, and wept over it. O Jerusalem, Jerusalem, thou that killest the prophets, and stonest them which are sent unto thee, how often would I have gathered thy children together, even as a hen gathereth her chickens under her wings, and ye would not.[4]

STORY OF THE AUTHOR AND THE HYMN: [5]

David, the shepherd boy of Israel, is known as the writer of the twenty-third psalm. The experiences of the days and nights spent with the flocks on the hills near Bethlehem fitted him to write this "Shepherd Psalm." In like manner the background of the youth of Dr. Frank Mason North enabled him to write the hymn of the city,

"Where Cross the Crowded Ways of Life." The streets of New York were as familiar to him as were the sheep paths of Judea to David. New York was to him an open book, for he spent much time in close contact with every phase of life of the jostling, moving crowds as they thronged the streets of the city.

After acquiring his college training at Wesleyan University, Middletown, Connecticut, Dr. North entered the ministry of the Methodist Church. While serving as pastor of several of the churches in New York City he was brought into contact with the many tragic problems of poverty, suffering, greed, exploitation, and racial strife. He saw every condition of life—the rich, the poor; the successful, the failures; the favored, the oppressed. He knew the needs and the longings of the multitudes as they crowded the streets of the city, and it was his sympathy for them which led him to write this hymn.

Dr. North had but one purpose in view when he wrote this hymn, and that was to help men of all races and conditions to understand better the person and the meaning of Jesus Christ. During his ministry, Jesus mingled with the throngs in the city, and they followed him to the wilderness and crowded about him when he desired to rest. One of the most touching incidents is the picture given by Matthew, depicting Jesus' grief as he looked over the Holy City of Jerusalem. Is it any wonder that Jesus wept as he thought of the problems of that city? He saw many things which troubled him: the weary and heavy laden as they longed for encouragement; the broken, frustrated lives of the downtrodden; and the dulled sensibilities and seared consciences of the careless leaders. In this agonizing cry of Jesus we catch a glimpse of what he must have suffered because of the sins of humanity.

In his hymn Dr. North has given us a twentieth-century version of Jesus weeping over a present-day city. "In haunts of wretchedness and need, on shadowed thresholds dark with fears, from paths where hide the lures of greed, we catch a vision of his tears." The spirit of Christ is sadly lacking in the clash of race and clan, in the strife and injustices.

> Where cross the crowded ways of life,
> Where sound the cries of race and clan,
> Above the noise of selfish strife,
> We hear thy voice, O Son of Man!

WHERE CROSS THE CROWDED WAYS OF LIFE

In haunts of wretchedness and need,
  On shadowed thresholds dark with fears,
From paths where hide the lures of greed,
  We catch the vision of thy tears.

From tender childhood's helpfulness,
  From woman's grief, man's burdened toil,
From famished souls, from sorrow's stress,
  Thy heart has never known recoil.

The cup of water given for thee
  Still holds the freshness of thy grace;
Yet long these multitudes to see
  The sweet compassion of thy face.

O Master, from the mountain side,
  Make haste to heal these hearts of pain;
Among the restless throngs abide,
  O tread the city's streets again,

Till sons of men shall learn thy love
  And follow where thy feet have trod;
Till, glorious from thy heaven above,
  Shall come the city of our God.
                          —FRANK MASON NORTH

POEM:

O Master of the multitude,
  Toilworn, dust-stained, and tanned,
The rich and poor, refined and rude,
  Of every time and land—
Come, walk with us and talk with us,
  And share our grief and woe;
O Master of the multitude,
  Teach us thy love to know.

O Master of the multitude,
  The millions wander still

Without a guide, without a light,
　　Without an aim or will—
Come, walk with us and talk with us
　　Among our people move;
O Master of the multitude,
　　Redeem us by thy love.[6]
　　　　　　　—CHAUNCEY R. PIETY

CLOSING PRAYER:

O thou Father of us all, draw all thy children together in a strong bond of love and fellowship. As thou didst reveal in thy Son a way of life for us to follow, help us to reflect in our lives the truths which the world beheld in Jesus. Purge from us any prejudice, hatred, strife, greed, or selfishness. Help us to love our fellow-men in such a manner that others may see thy love reflected in us. Open our eyes to the needs of those about us; save us from snobbishness or class hatred; deliver us from an economic system which puts profits above personality. Increase our faith in a better social order, and may we have the grace to bring it about by moral means. In Jesus' name we pray. AMEN.

BENEDICTION:

May the love of God remain with you both now and forever. AMEN.

SERVICE 26

ALL CREATURES OF OUR GOD AND KING

(*St. Francis of Assisi*)

AIM: To help the group to find joy through a discovery of God as revealed in nature.

PRELUDE: "Simple Confession" by Francis Thome.

CALL TO WORSHIP:

> God of the glorious sunshine,
>   God of refreshing rain,
> Whose voice bids earth awaken
>   And clothe itself again.
> With life of richest beauty
>   In plant, in flower, and tree;
> Thou God of light and splendor,
>   We rise and worship thee.
>
> God of hill and mountain,
>   Of valley and of dale,
> Whose finger paints the rainbows;
>   Thy beauties never fail
> To raise our souls in wonder,
>   And turn our thoughts to thee;
> Thou God of living nature,
>   We stand and worship thee.
>   —THOMAS PAXTON

HYMN: "Joyful, Joyful, We Adore Thee," or
"Bring, O Morn, Thy Music."

RESPONSIVE READING:

Leader: The Lord reigneth, let the earth rejoice; let the multitude of isles be glad thereof.

Group: The sun is on the land and sea,
  The day begun;
Our morning hymn begins with thee,
  Blest Three in One;
Our praise shall rise continually
  Till day is done.

Leader: The Lord hath done great things for us; whereof we are glad.

Group: Thy love was ever in our view,
  Like stars by night;
Thy gifts are every morning new,
  O God of light;
Thy mercy, like the heavens' blue,
  Fills all our sight.

Leader: Weeping may endure for a night, but joy cometh in the morning.

Group: We do not know what grief or care
  The day may bring:
The heart shall find some gladness there
  That loves its King;
The life that serves thee everywhere
  Can always sing.

Leader: He hath made everything beautiful in his time: also he hath set the world in their heart.

Group: All glory to the Father be,
  With Christ the Son,
And, Holy Spirit, unto thee,
  Forever One;
All glory to the Trinity
  While ages run! [1]

ALL CREATURES OF OUR GOD AND KING

Our Father, we thank thee for the universe which thou hast created. Open our eyes that the glories of nature may ever remind us of thee. Unstop our ears that every voice of wood and stream may speak thy message to us. Quicken our minds that we may understand that the beauty which we see is an expression of thy love for us. We praise thee for the beauty which we see all about us. Help us to become more worthy of thy goodness. In Jesus' name. AMEN.

POEM.

At evening along some sea
I walk to watch an ancient tree
Where gently, at the close of day,
It bows its hallowed head to pray.

There is a vesper hour for trees,
    There is an Angelus which rings
With sweetest music through the leaves,
    An evening wind which softly sings.

Whoever will, may hear this prayer
    Who walks along some sundown sea.
Or through a forest anywhere
    And stands at sunset by a tree.

Stand all alone and silently,
In prayerful mood and reverently;
Then you will hear that priestly tree
At vespers praying wistfully.

You'll hear a whisper soft and low,
    You'll hear one speaking tenderly,
And through the wandering winds which blow,
    You'll hear God talking to that tree.

You'll feel a touch of timeless things,
    You'll feel a sense of reverence steal
Across your soul, while silence clings
    Where on God's grass of green you kneel.[2]

—WILLIAM L. STIDGER

HYMNS

St. Francis, the writer of the hymn, "All Creatures of Our God and King," was born in the town of Assisi in central Italy in the year 1182. He grew to manhood in this beautiful little town high in the Appennine Mountains, overlooking the Umbrian plains. As the son of a wealthy cloth merchant, he lived a gay and luxurious life; he dressed in gorgeous silks and threw his money about in reckless extravagance. More like a prince than the son of a merchant was he. At heart he was a troubadour, for he enjoyed strolling along the streets with his companions, singing the songs of his native country. But when he reached manhood, even in the midst of luxurious surroundings he became dissatisfied.

All efforts to make a merchant of Francis were utter failures. On one occasion when he was engaged in selling a bolt of cloth to a customer, a beggar came beseeching alms. By the time the deal was closed, the beggar had disappeared in the crowd. Francis, leaving his goods unprotected, raced through the narrow streets after the beggar, and upon finding him, gave the poor creature more money than he had ever seen before. Ofttimes Francis was rash and impractical, but in his dealings with people he was at all times kind and considerate.

After a while the streets of Assisi were quiet; the song of the troubadour was heard no more, for Francis had gone with a company of lancers to fight for his country. His career as a soldier was brief, for he was taken captive and later contracted a fever which lasted for many weeks. When, at last, he recovered sufficiently to go home, he felt a great desire to see the beautiful country around Assisi, but his return brought him no joy. He looked upon the broad Umbrian plain, saw the purple haze resting upon the beautiful mountains, and felt sick at heart.

Francis lacked inner peace and was disturbed by the question of what he should do with the remainder of his life. He was eager to invest it where it would count for the most, but there was nothing open to him except fighting for his country. So off he rode to war, but before he had gone very far, fever seized him again. As he was recovering from this illness, a voice spoke to him as in a dream, saying, "Return to your home and it shall be shown you what you shall do."

Immediately upon his return, Francis went to the village church which he found neglected and falling to pieces. As he knelt in prayer

a voice seemed to say, "My Church is in ruins; go, restore it for me."
He wanted to use his father's money in rebuilding the church, but
the father had no sympathy with his son's new idea. Then all at
once like a flash a vision came to him, and he beheld what love had
led Jesus to do. The way ahead was not clear, but from that time
forward he determined that love should rule his life also. He tried to
tell his father of his decision, but the father was unable to understand.

Casting off his rich clothes and donning a coarse gray robe, Francis
set out to be a brother to the poor, serving wherever there was need.
He wandered over Italy, living a life of extreme poverty. His simplicity
and humility appealed to the people. In a short while men in other
countries caught the spirit of his unselfish life and were following him
in the way of obedience and self-denial. In less than ten years there
were more than five thousand Franciscans, or "Gray Friars," who had
donned the gray peasant's robe and dedicated themselves to a life of
service. Never had Europe seen so clear a vision of the love of Jesus
as was shown by members of this brotherhood which Francis founded.

As he tramped about the country, a peace and joy which he had
never known before came to Francis. In becoming God's Troubadour
he found more joy than he had ever known in his youth. The simple,
commonplace things of life brought him great happiness: little wild
creatures of the forest seemed to know him; birds sang their gayest
songs for him; and the out-of-doors was to him the gift of his Heavenly
Father, the Creator of all beauty.

Shortly before his death, as Francis lay in his hut, ill and blind,
the words of the hymn "All Creatures of Our God and King"
came to him. No doubt he had been meditating upon a psalm of
praise, perhaps the one hundred forty-fifth, when the lines formed
themselves in his mind. As we read the hymn, we think of it as being
written in pleasant surroundings, in the midst of beauty. Instead,
the writer was desperately ill, distressed by excessive heat, and tormented by field mice as they ran over his body. But Francis had
so much joy stored up within him that he could write in a joyous
manner in any situation. Out of his suffering and discomfort, he
has created a hymn of such beauty that the passing of time has not
affected it in the least. More than seven hundred years have passed
since the writing of the hymn, and it is still a favorite with young
people.

All creatures of our God and King,
Lift up your voice and with us sing
  Alleluia! Alleluia!
Thou burning sun with golden beam,
Thou silver moon with softer gleam!
  O praise him! Alleluia!

Thou rushing wind that art so strong,
Ye clouds that sail in heaven along,
  O praise him! Alleluia!
Thou rising morn, in praise rejoice,
Ye lights of evening, find a voice!
  O praise him! Alleluia!

Thou flowing water, pure and clear,
Make music for thy Lord to hear,
  Alleluia! Alleluia!
Thou fire so masterful and bright,
Thou givest man both warmth and light!
  O praise him! Alleluia!

Dear mother earth, who day by day
Unfoldest blessings on our way,
  O praise him! Alleluia!
The flowers and fruits that in thee grow,
Let them his glory also show!
  O praise him! Alleluia!

And all ye men of tender heart,
Forgiving others, take your part
  O sing ye! Alleluia!
Ye who long pain and sorrow bear,
Praise God and on him cast your care!
  O praise him! Alleluia!

Let all things their Creator bless,
And worship him in humbleness,
  O praise him! Alleluia!

Praise, praise the Father, praise the Son,
And praise the Spirit, Three in One!
O praise him!   Alleluia!
—St. Francis of Assisi

PRAYER:

Our Father, we come to thee with praise upon our lips for the beauty which we see about us everywhere. Grant that as we meditate upon thy goodness we may strive to live according to thy purpose for us. Grant that an appreciation of the beauty in nature may lead us to make our lives beautiful too. Help us to become more sensitive to the revelations of thyself in the world which thou hast created. As we think of followers of thine who have lived according to thy purpose, help us to choose the way of service and self-denial. In Jesus' name. AMEN.

BENEDICTION:

The Lord of earth and sea and skies,
To whom our reverent praises rise,
With light and love our spirits fill,
As we go forth to do thy will. AMEN.
—EDWIN RALPH

SERVICE 27

IN CHRIST THERE IS NO EAST OR WEST

(John Oxenham)

AIM: To help the group to have an attitude of friendliness toward all races of people.

PRELUDE: Hymn tune "Mozart."

CALL TO WORSHIP:

Make a joyful noise unto the Lord, all ye lands.

Serve the Lord with gladness; come before his presence with singing.

Know ye that the Lord he is God; it is he that made us, and not we ourselves: we are his people, and the sheep of his pasture.

Enter into his gates with thanksgiving, and into his courts with praise: be thankful unto him, and bless his name.

For the Lord is good, his mercy is everlasting; and his truth endureth to all generations.[1]

HYMN: "Jesus Shall Reign," or
      "Lift Up Our Hearts."

LITANY OF BROTHERHOOD:

Leader: Then Peter said, Of a truth I perceive that God is no respecter of persons: but in every nation he that feareth him, and worketh righteousness, is accepted with him.

Group: At length there dawns the glorious day
    By prophets long foretold,
At length the chorus clearer grows
    That shepherds heard of old,

The day of dawning brotherhood
   Breaks on our eager eyes,
And human hatreds flee before
   The radiant eastern skies.

Leader: For he is our peace, who hath made both one, and hath broken
down the middle wall of partition between us; for through
him we both have access by one Spirit unto the Father.

Group: For what are sundering strains of blood,
   Or ancient caste and creed?
One claim unites all men in God
   To serve each human need.
Then here together, brother men,
. We pledge the Lord anew
Our loyal love, our stalwart faith,
   Our service strong and true.

Leader: Now therefore ye are no more strangers and foreigners, but
fellow-citizens with the saints, and of the household of God.

Group: One common faith unites us all,
   We seek one common goal;
One tender comfort broods upon
   The struggling human soul.
To this clear call of brotherhood
   Our hearts responsive ring;
We join the glorious new crusade
   Of our great Lord and King.[2]

PRAYER:

We thank thee, O God, for the long succession of thy singers who
have lifted thy people's hearts and brightened their way with music;
and we pray that we also may learn to greet the hard places of life
with a song, and climbing steadfastly may enter into the fellowship of
thy white-robed choristers in heaven; through Jesus Christ our Lord.
AMEN.[3]

HYMN: "O Brother Man, Fold to Thy Heart."

POEM:

     We can never build God's Kingdom
     Till we learn to love man more,

Till we trample the injustice
   That now tramples down the poor;

Till employers and employees
   Stifle selfish greed and strife,
And co-operate as brothers
   As they seek abundant life;

Till we banish brutal passions
   That make armies, navies, wars;
Till we conquer racial hatreds,
   And break down the color bars.

We can never build God's Kingdom
   In a corner by itself;
It must master earth and mankind,
   Social orders, power, and pelf.[4]
       —CHAUNCEY R. PIETY

STORY OF THE AUTHOR AND THE HYMN:

John Oxenham, the author of this hymn, is an outstanding poet and writer of England today. Following his college days at Victoria University, Manchester, he entered business which led him to travel extensively over Europe, Canada, and the United States. At one time he visited the South, thinking he would settle in Georgia as a sheep-raiser or in Florida as an orange-grower. But after careful consideration and observation he decided that these occupations were precarious, and returned to his home in England.

The British *Who's Who* states that he took up writing as an alternative from business and, finding it more enjoyable, dropped business and stuck to writing. During the last thirty years he has published more than twenty volumes of verse and fifty novels, in addition to his books of a religious nature, such as *The Hidden Years*. Of his books of verse more than a million copies have been sold. His best known poem, "The High Way," has become such a favorite that it has been set to music and is now used in many young people's meetings.

In 1908 the London Missionary Society asked Mr. Oxenham to write a missionary pageant for them. In answer to their request he produced "Darkness and Light." This pageant was used widely for a number of years in England and America, where it was seen by thousands of people. The lines of the hymn, "In Christ There Is No East or West," were written to combine two parts of the pageant. Mr. Oxenham had no thought of contributing to hymnody when he wrote these lines; but he has produced a hymn of such worth that it appears in many hymn books all over the world, and has been translated into several languages, including the Chinese and Japanese.

Mr. Oxenham has shown evidence of deep spiritual insight and close contact with the divine in the thought expressed in this hymn. He points to the new day which will come when there is "one great fellowship of love throughout the whole wide earth." Since science has lessened the distances between nations and has made the world a neighborhood, it now remains for the followers of Christ to make it a brotherhood. That day will come when Christians rightly interpret Jesus' teachings on the worth of human personality and show in their relations one with the other the meaning of brotherhood. Young people in many countries are singing that he "who serves my Father as a son is surely kin to me," and gradually a consciousness of the great fellowship of love is dawning throughout the earth.

HYMN:

> In Christ there is no East or West,
>   In him no South or North;
> But one great fellowship of love
>   Throughout the whole wide earth.

> In him shall true hearts everywhere
>   Their high communion find;
> His service is the golden cord
>   Close binding all mankind.

> Join hands, then, brothers of the faith,
>   Whate'er your race may be
> Who serves my Father as a son
>   Is surely kin to me.

> In Christ now meet both East and West,
>   In him meet South and North;

All Christly souls are one in him
Throughout the whole wide earth.[5]
—John Oxenham

AN AFFIRMATION OF FAITH:

I affirm my faith in the Kingdom of God and my hope in its final triumph. I determine by faith to live day by day within the higher order and the divine peace of my true Fatherland, and to carry its spirit and laws into all my dealings in the world that now is.

I make an act of love toward all my fellowmen. I accept them as they are, with all their sins and failures, and declare my solidarity with them. If any have wronged or grieved me, I place my mind within the all-comprehending and all-loving mind of God, and here and now forgive. I desire to minister God's love to men and to offer no hindrance to the free flow of his love through me.

I affirm my faith in life. I call life good and not evil. I accept the limitations of my own life and believe it is possible for me to live a beautiful and Christlike life within the conditions set for me. Through the power of Christ which descends on me, I know that I can be more than conqueror. AMEN.[6]

POEM:

Who is so low that I am not his brother?
  Who is so high that I've no path to him?
Who is so poor I may not feel his hunger?
  Who is so rich I may not pity him?

Who is so hurt I may not know his heartache?
  Who sings for joy my heart may never share?
Who in God's heaven has passed beyond my vision?
  Who to hell's depths where I may never fare?

May none, then, call on me for understanding,
  May none, then, turn to me for help in pain,
And drain alone his bitter cup of sorrow,
  Or find he knocks upon my heart in vain.[7]
—S. Ralph Harlow

PRAYER:

O God, our Father, King of the whole earth, break down, we beseech thee, by thy great power, all those barriers which do now keep mankind asunder; overcome the hindrances of race, of custom, and of prejudice; drive out all those adverse influences which now mar our union. Foster throughout the world every movement of thought, of activity, of goodwill, which tends, for whatever motive and in whatever sphere, to break down isolation and exclusiveness, to unite men in common enterprise and service, to build up co-operation and inter-dependence. AMEN.[8]

BENEDICTION:

May the peace of God abide in your hearts, and the word of Christ dwell in you richly in all wisdom. AMEN.

SERVICE 28

O YOUNG AND FEARLESS PROPHET
(S. Ralph Harlow)

AIM: To lead the group to commit themselves to the truths which Christ taught.

PRELUDE: "Andante" from *Sonata in G* by Beethoven.

CALL TO WORSHIP:

> As with gladness men of old
> Did the guiding star behold;
> As with joy they hailed its light,
> Leading onward, beaming bright;
> So, most gracious Lord, may we
> Evermore be led to thee.
>
> As they offered gifts most rare,
> At that manger rude and bare,
> So may we with holy joy,
> Pure and free from sin's alloy,
> All our costliest treasures bring,
> Christ, to thee, our heavenly King.
> —WILLIAM C. DIX

HYMN: "Christ of the Upward Way," or
"Breathe on Me, Breath of God."

RESPONSIVE READING:

Leader: Let this mind be in you, which was also in Christ Jesus:

Group: Who, being in the form of God, thought it not robbery to be equal with God;

Leader: But made himself of no reputation, and took upon him the form of a servant, and was made in the likeness of men:

Group: And being found in fashion as a man, he humbled himself, and became obedient unto death, even the death of the cross.

Leader: Wherefore God also hath highly exalted him, and given him a name which is above every name:

Group: That at the name of Jesus every knee should bow, of things in heaven, and things in earth, and things under the earth;

Leader: And that every tongue should confess that Jesus Christ is Lord, to the glory of God the Father.

Group: For it is God which worketh in you both to will and to do of his good pleasure.[1]

DIRECTED MEDITATION:

Let us think of Jesus, as he faced the ignorance and superstition of his day, saying, "I am the truth."

> O Thou whose feet have climbed life's hill,
>   And trod the path of youth,
> Our Saviour and our Brother still,
>   Now lead us into truth.

In the midst of the hypocrisy and the religious formalism of his day, he said, "I am the way."

> The call is thine: be thou the Way,
>   And give us men to guide;
> Let wisdom broaden with the day,
>   Let human faith abide.

In the midst of intrenched wrong, oppression, and greed, he said, "I am the truth."

> Who learn of thee the truth shall find,
>   Who follow, gain the goal;
> With reverence crown the earnest mind,
>   And speak within the soul.

In the midst of hatred and prejudice, brother striving against brother, he said, "I am the truth."

> Awake the purpose high which strives,
> And, falling, stands again;
> Confirm the will of eager lives
> To quit themselves like men.

In the midst of a society which placed material values above human vaules, he said, "I am the way, the truth, the light."

> Thy life the bond of fellowship,
> Thy love the law that rules,
> Thy name, proclaimed by every lip,
> The Master of our schools.[2]

HYMN: "O Jesus, Youth of Nazareth," or
　　　"Fairest Lord Jesus."

STORY:

There was once a man who was born in an obscure village, the child of a peasant woman. He grew to manhood in another obscure village—a despised one. The family was very poor; and when the father died, the boy took his father's place and supported his mother and family. He worked in a carpenter shop until he was thirty, and then for three years was an itinerant minister. His short ministry was spent about the shores of one small lake, never having traveled two hundred miles from the place where he was born. He walked among men and touched their lives; his few intimate friends were lowly fishermen. He never wrote a book, or won earthly fame; he never held an office, or owned a home, or possessed material wealth; he never went to college, or did one of the things that usually accompanies greatness.

While still a young man, the tide of popular opinion turned against him. His friends ran away, one of them denying him. His own people rejected him, turning him over to his enemies. He went through the mockery of a trial. Although guiltless, he was nailed upon a cross between two thieves. His executioners gambled for the only piece of property he had on earth—his seamless robe. When he was dead he was taken from the cross and laid in a borrowed grave through the courtesy of a friend.

O YOUNG AND FEARLESS PROPHET

Nineteen centuries have come and gone, and I am far within the mark when I say that all the armies that ever marched, all the navies that ever were built, all the parliaments that ever sat, and all the kings that ever reigned, put together have not affected the life of man as powerfully as has that *one solitary life*.[3]

POEM:

> Jesus, whose lot with us was cast,
> Who saw it out, from first to last:
> Patient, fearless, tender, true,
> Carpenter, vagabond, felon, Jew:
> Whose humorous eye took in each phase
> Of full, rich life this world displays,
> Yet evermore kept fast in view
> The far-off goal it leads us to:
> Who, as your hour neared, did not fail—
> The world's fate trembling in the scale—
> With your half-hearted band to dine,
> And chat across the bread and wine:
> Then went out firm to face the end,
> Alone, without a single friend:
> Who felt, as your last words confessed,
> Wrung from a proud unflinching breast
> By hours of dull ignoble pain,
> Your whole life's fight was fought in vain:
> Would I could win and keep and feel
> That heart of love, that spirit of steel.
>
> —AUTHOR UNKNOWN

STORY OF THE HYMN:

While motoring through the country in the state of Massachusetts, Dr. Ralph Harlow remarked to his wife, "The lines of a hymn are coming to me with no effort on my part; the engine of this car seems to be chugging out the words." Stopping for lunch a few moments later, Mrs. Harlow suggested, "Ralph, don't you think it would be well to write out those lines before they leave you?" Picking up a menu card, he scribbled the lines on the back of the card and passed it to his wife to read.

Continuing their journey, they passed a brook in which a man was bathing his feet. Mrs. Harlow remarked about the tired expression on the man's face. As they began the ascent of a rather steep hill, the thought of the tired man kept coming back to them. Finally Mrs. Harlow remarked, "Do you know, Ralph, that if we really believed what you wrote in those verses, we would turn back and give that man a lift." Although they were halfway up the hill, they turned around, drove back to the brook, and invited the man to ride with them.

They drew from the man his story: Leaving a sick wife in Boston, he had walked several hundred miles in search of work. Everywhere he got the same answer—there were scores ahead of him waiting for every opening. Being too proud to beg, the man was actually starving. His story closed with the remark, "Just as I thought God had forgotten me this happened. I was thinking of suicide when you came along."

Work was secured for the man, who is at the present time contented and living a useful life.

When the lines of the hymn "O Young and Fearless Prophet" were set to music and included in a hymnal for the first time one stanza was omitted. It so happened that it was the stanza to which Mrs. Harlow had referred as they turned around to give the man a lift. We wonder if the committee in omitting the fourth stanza felt that Christians were not ready to sing the words.

HYMN:

> O young and fearless Prophet of ancient Galilee:
> Thy life is still a summons to serve humanity,
> To make our thoughts and actions less prone to please the crowd,
> To stand with humble courage for Truth with hearts uncowed.
>
> We marvel at the purpose that held thee to thy course
> While ever on the hilltop before thee loomed the cross;
> Thy steadfast face set forward where love and duty shone,
> While we betray so quickly and leave thee there alone.
>
> O help us stand unswerving against war's bloody way,
> Where hate and lust and falsehood hold back Christ's holy sway;
> Forbid false love of country, that blinds us to his call
> Who lifts above the nation the brotherhood of all.

O YOUNG AND FEARLESS PROPHET

Stir up in us a protest against the greed of wealth,
While men go crushed and hungry, who plead for work and
 health,
Whose wives and little children cry out for lack of bread,
Who spend their years o'erweighted beneath a gloomy dread.

Create in us the splendor that dawns when hearts are kind,
That knows not race nor station as boundaries of the mind;
That learns to value beauty, in heart, or brain, or soul,
And longs to bind God's children into one perfect whole.

O young and fearless Prophet, we need thy presence here,
Amid our pride and glory to see thy face appear;
Once more to hear thy challenge above our noisy day,
Again to lead us forward along God's holy way.[4]

—S. RALPH HARLOW

LITANY OF SUPPLICATION:

Leader: O thou divine Son of God who came into the world to reveal
 the Father,

Group: Open our eyes that we may see God in thee.

Leader: O thou Guide and Revealer of truth,

Group: Grant that we may be aware of thy presence and feel strangely
 drawn to thee.

Leader: O thou divine Wayfarer whose first shelter was a stable,

Group: Make us sensitive to thy invitation, "Come unto me, and I
 will give you rest."

Leader: O thou divine Son of Toil who labored unceasingly,

Group: Strengthen those of us who also toil for our daily bread.

Leader: O thou divine Companion of the Road who trod the highways
 carrying the good news to those who sat in darkness,

Group: We would dedicate ourselves to the task of spreading thy
 gospel.

Leader: O thou Saviour of mankind who saith, "And I, if I be lifted up
 will draw all men unto me."

Group: Grant that we may catch the significance of this truth and lift thee up in our lives.

Leader: O thou divine Son of God, as thy voice echoes across the centuries saying, "For this cause came I into the world, that I might witness to the truth."

Group: Help us to catch thy spirit and pattern our lives according to thy truth. In thy name. AMEN.

BENEDICTION:

The Lord bless you and keep you: the Lord make his face to shine upon you and be gracious unto you: the Lord lift up his countenance upon you and give you peace. AMEN.

SERVICE 29

LIFT EVERY VOICE AND SING
(James Weldon Johnson)

AIM: To lead to a better understanding of the longing of the Negro to express himself and to rise to greater heights.

PRELUDE: Music to spiritual "Swing Low, Sweet Chariot."

CALL TO WORSHIP:

> Brother, come!
> And let us go unto our God.
> And when we stand before him
> I shall say—
> "Lord, I do not hate,
> I am hated.
> I scourge no one,
> I am scourged.
> I covet no lands,
> My lands are coveted.
> I mock no people,
> My people are mocked."
> And brother, what shall you say? [1]
> —JOSEPH SEAMON COTTER, JR.

HYMN: Spiritual "Steal Away to Jesus," or
"Standing in the Need of Prayer."

SCRIPTURE:

If we say that we have no sin, we deceive ourselves, and the truth is not in us. If we confess our sins, he is faithful and just to forgive us our sins, and to clease us from all unrighteousness.

He hath not dealt with us after our sins, nor rewarded us according to our iniquities. For as the heaven is high above the earth so great is his mercy toward them that fear him. As far as the east is from the west, so far hath he removed our transgressions from us.

Then came Peter to him and said, Lord, how oft shall my brother sin against me, and I forgive him? Till seven times? Jesus saith unto him, I say not unto thee, Until seven times; but, Until seventy times seven.[2]

PRAYER:

Our Father, we come to thee in deep humility as we think of the fear and distrust between races. Forgive us for every thought, word, or deed which we have committed that would separate thy human family. Forgive our lack of understanding of each other—our distrust, false pride, or self-conceit. If we have made life harder for any of our brothers, help them to forgive us. Grant that we do not allow prejudice to blight our life. Increase our faith in the power of love and good will. In Jesus' name. AMEN.

SPIRITUAL: "Lord, I Want to Be a Christian."

POEM:

> To be a Negro in a day like this
>   Demands forgiveness. Bruised with blow on blow,
> Betrayed, like him whose woe-dimmed eyes gave bliss,
>   Still must one succor those who brought one low,
> To be a Negro in a day like this.
>
> To be a Negro in a day like this.
>   Demands rare patience—patience that can wait
> In utter darkness. 'Tis the path to miss,
>   And knock, unheeded, at an iron gate,
> To be a Negro in a day like this.
>
> To be a Negro in a day like this
>   Demands strange loyalty. We serve a flag
> Which is to us white freedom's emphasis.

> Ah! one must love when Truth and Justice lag,
> To be a Negro in a day like this.
>
> To be a Negro in a day like this—
>   Alas! Lord God, what evil have we done?
> Still shines the gate, all gold and amethyst,
>   But I pass by, the glorious goal unwon,
> "Merely a Negro"—in a day like this! [3]
>   —JAMES DAVID CORROTHERS

STORY OF THE AUTHOR AND THE HYMN:

James Weldon Johnson, the Negro poet and writer, was born in Jacksonville, Florida, and was educated in the public schools of that city and at Atlanta University. He did graduate work at Columbia University and had conferred upon him the honorary degree of Doctor of Literature from Talladega College and Howard University. For several years, while serving as principal of a high school in Jacksonville, he continued his study of law and passed the bar examination, but practised only a short while. Later he went to New York to collaborate with his brother, J. Rosamond Johnson, in writing for light opera stage. He wrote the words while his brother composed the music— a project which proved a financial success. But the writing of popular songs to amuse people did not satisfy his desire for higher aspirations, and he turned to a more serious type of writing.

Soon after the turn of the century Mr. Johnson was sent as United States consul to Venezuela, and later to Nicaragua, a more difficult post. He was a consul through three revolutions and won especially the gratitude of the Americans whose lives and property were in danger. When he returned home as a private citizen, the difference accorded him in treatment was quite noticeable. As a consul he had been received by rulers as the representative of a great republic, and his accomplishments as a scholar had been recognized. But in his native land he was handicapped and had to undergo injustices which he thought no longer existed.

Retiring for a time, Mr. Johnson wrote his first novel, *Autobiography of an Ex-colored Man,* which he published anonymously, though it was brought out later under his own name. Although it was written as fiction, his own experiences were drawn upon as much as he desired. In it he interpreted the feeling of his own race regarding the limitations and restriction placed upon them. He was drawn into public life again and served for fourteen years as secretary of the National Association for the Advancement of Colored People. During this time he was awarded the Spingarn Medal for the most distinguished service rendered by a member of his race.

What seemed to him a real opportunity came when he was called to the chair of creative literature at Fisk University, a position which he held until his death. As he touched the lives of Negro youth, his purpose was to help them come to a clearer understanding of the contribution they could make to the nation of which they were a part. He had a firm conviction that the Negro should no longer be thought of as a receiver, a burden, and a liability waiting to be thrown the crumbs of civilization. He said, "The easily found-out truth is that the Negro is and has long been a giver as well as a receiver, a creator as well as a creature; that he is and has long been a vital force in the making of America."

Mr. Johnson was one of the most prolific of the Negro writers. He brought out a collection of his own poems, two volumes of spirituals, and an anthology, *The Book of American Negro Poetry,* which is the most complete in its field. His autobiography, *Along This Way,* in which he gives the account of a full and varied career, has attracted wide and favorable attention. In it are to be found many interesting sidelights on Paul Lawrence Dunbar, Madame Schumann-Heink, Woodrow Wilson, and others.

In his "Creation," from *God's Trombones,* Mr. Johnson gives one of his best poems. In it he has given a lofty conception of God which does not fail to grip the emotions. God is pictured as stepping out in space while he creates the world, clothing it with beauty, and peopling it with the lower forms of life. Then God looks upon it all and sees that it is good, but he is lonely still. He closes with an appealing picture of God seeking human companionship, yearning for the love of his children; and so "God made man in his own image and likeness."

Of his writings an early poem is the one by which he is best remembered. It was his song of aspiration written while he was principal of the high school in Jacksonville. It was composed for a group of school children to sing at the celebration of Lincoln's birthday. His brother wrote the music. Today it is known as the Negro National Anthem and is sung throughout the country.

In this song, "Lift Every Voice and Sing," he has brought to our attention the longings of his own race, their desire for freedom and self-expression. He portrays the spirit of youth, which is the same in all climes and in all ages—a youth that continues to struggle in the face of great odds. There is something within him that soars above race and touched the heart universal. As we sing this song let us visualize the suffering of the race as it turns its sorrow into a song, making music the weapon of its resistance.

Negro National Anthem:

>Lift every voice and sing
>Till earth and heaven ring,
>Ring with the harmonies of Liberty;
>Let our rejoicing rise
>High as the list'ning skies,
>Let it resound loud as the rolling sea;
>Sing a song full of the faith that the dark past has taught us;
>Sing a song full of the hope that the present has brought us;
>Facing the rising sun
>Of our new day begun
>Let us march on till victory is won.

>Stony the road we trod,
>Bitter the chast'ning rod
>Felt in the days when hope unborn had died;
>Yet with a steady beat,
>Have not our weary feet
>Come to the place for which our fathers sighed?
>We have come over a way that with tears has been watered,
>We have come, treading our path through the blood of the
> slaughtered,
>Out of the gloomy past,
>Till now we stand at last
>Where the white gleam of our bright star is cast.

>God of our weary years,
>God of our silent tears,
>Thou who hast brought us thus far on the way;
>Thou who hast by thy might,

Led us into the light,
Keep us forever in the path, we pray,
Lest our feet stray from the places, our God, where we met thee,
Lest, our hearts drunk with the wine of the world, we forget thee;
Shadowed beneath thy hand,
May we forever stand,
True to our God, true to our Native Land.[4]

—JAMES WELDON JOHNSON

PRAYER:

God of all nations,
We pray thee for all the peoples of thy earth:
For those who are consumed in mutual hatred and bitterness:
For those who make bloody war upon their neighbours:
For those who tyrannously oppress:
For those who groan under cruelty and subjection.

We pray thee for all those who bear rule and responsibility:
For child-races and dying races:
For outcaste tribes, the backward and the downtrodden:
For the ignorant, the wretched, the enslaved.

We beseech thee to teach mankind to live together in peace:
No man exploiting the weak, no man hating the strong,
Each race working out its own destiny,
Unfettered, self-respecting, fearless.

Teach us to be worthy of freedom,
Free from social wrong, free from individual oppression and contempt,
Pure of heart and hand, despising none, defrauding none,
Giving to all men—in all the dealings of life—
The honour we owe to those who are thy children,
Whatever their colour, their race or their caste. AMEN.[5]

BENEDICTION:

May the spirit of Christ abide with you now and forever. AMEN.

SERVICE 30

RISE UP, O MEN OF GOD

(William P. Merrill)

Aɪᴍ: To lead to a better understanding of the meaning of brotherhood.

Pʀᴇʟᴜᴅᴇ: Hymn Tune "St. Thomas."

Cᴀʟʟ ᴛᴏ Wᴏʀsʜɪᴘ:

> Lord, speak to me, that I may speak
>   In living echoes of thy tone;
> As thou hast sought, so let me seek
>   Thine erring children lost and lone.
>
> O fill me with thy fullness, Lord,
>   Until my very heart o'erflow
> In kindling thought and glowing word,
>   Thy love to tell, thy praise to show.
>   —Fʀᴀɴᴄᴇs R. Hᴀᴠᴇʀɢᴀʟ

Pʀᴀʏᴇʀ Hʏᴍɴ: "O Son of Man, Thou Madest Known," or
              "O Jesus, Master, When Today."

Rᴇsᴘᴏɴsɪᴠᴇ Rᴇᴀᴅɪɴɢ:

Leader: And it shall come to pass in the last days, saith God, that I
       will pour out of my Spirit on all flesh.

Group: Our Fathers' God, from out whose hand
       The centuries fall like grains of sand,
       We meet today, united, free,
       And loyal to our land and thee,

To thank thee for the era done,
And trust thee for the opening one.

Leader: And they shall not teach every man his neighbor, and every
man his brother, saying, Know the Lord: for all shall know
me, from the least to the greatest.

Group: For art and labor met in truce,
For beauty made the bride of use,
We thank thee; but, withal, we crave
The austere virtues strong to save,
The honor proof to place or gold,
The manhood never bought nor sold!

Leader: And they shall come from the east, and from the west, and
from the north, and from the south, and shall sit down in the
kingdom of God. For it is not the will of our Father which
is in heaven, that one of these little ones should perish.

Group: O, make us, through the centuries long,
In peace secure, in justice strong;
Around our gift of freedom draw
The safeguards of thy righteous law;
And, cast in some diviner mold,
Let the new cycle shame the old! [1]

HYMN:

America! America!
The shouts of war shall cease;
The Glory dawns! The Day is come
Of Victory and Peace!
And now upon a larger plan
We'll build the common good,
The temple of the Love of Man,
The House of Brotherhood!

What though its stones were laid in tears,
Its pillars red with wrong,
Its walls shall rise through patient years
To soaring spires of song!
For on this House shall Faith attend

With Joy on airy wing,
And flaming loyalty ascend
To God, the only King!

America! America!
Ring out the glad refrain!
Salute the Flag—salute the dead
That have not died in vain!
O glory, glory to thy plan
To build the common good,
The temple of the Rights of Man,
The House of Brotherhood! [2]

—ALLEN EASTMAN CROSS

SCRIPTURE:

Watch ye, stand fast in the faith, quit you like men, be strong.[3]

INTERPRETATION OF THE HYMN:

Dr. William P. Merrill, the author of the hymn "Rise Up, O Men of God," is pastor emeritus of the Brick Presbyterian Church on Fifth Avenue in New York City. He has long been one of the outstanding ministers of this generation who has kept pace with advancing thought and changing conditions.

Although Dr. Merrill wrote this hymn nearly thirty years ago, it has a timely message for our own day. As we study the lines of the hymn we are reminded of Micah's statement, "What doth the Lord require of thee, but to do justly, to love mercy, and to walk humbly with thy God." In these days of social injustice, greed, and oppression, there is need to recognize the importance of human values as over against material values.

At the beginning of the "machine age" John Ruskin wrote, "The great cry that goes up from our manufacturing cities is that we manufacture everything but man. We blanch cotton, refine sugar, strengthen steel, shape pottery, but to strengthen or to refine or to shape a single human soul does not enter into our estimate of advantages." Although much progress has been made in bringing about social justice since Ruskin's day, much remains yet to be done. We recognize the need for improved social conditions, but how is it to be accomplished?

Speaking before a group on one occasion Dr. Channing Tobias suggested a remedy which is definitely related to the message of this hymn. He said, "It is not problems that we need to solve, but attitudes. Give me two men with proper attitudes, and I care not how complex the problem, they will reach a satisfactory solution. It is useless even for us to talk of the solution to our problems. There will be no solution if by that you mean the final answer to our questions. For if we should solve every question of today, tomorrow would present us with new ones. Hence in my lifetime I do not expect to see a solution to our problems. I came and found them; I shall go and leave them. The best for which I can hope is that those who follow where I have trod will find the way a bit easier to travel because I have been there before them."

In the hymn Dr. Merrill brings the same message but in a different manner. He points out the fact that the kingdom will tarry until our attitudes are changed and we learn to live as brothers with all men. Some of the ills are so deeply intrenched that it will not be an easy matter to uproot them. The call goes out to young people to adventure with Christ in bringing about social justice, friendship among races, and good will among nations.

HYMN:

> Rise up, O men of God!
>   Have done with lesser things;
> Give heart and mind and soul and strength
>   To serve the King of kings.
>
> Rise up, O men of God!
>   His kingdom tarries long;
> Bring in the day of brotherhood
>   And end the night of wrong.
>
> Rise up, O men of God!
>   The Church for you doth wait,
> Her strength unequal to her task;
>   Rise up, and make her great!
>
> Lift high the cross of Christ!
>   Tread where his feet have trod;

As brothers of the Son of Man,
Rise up, O men of God! [4]
                    —WILLIAM PIERSON MERRILL

PRAYER:

Our Father, we know that the hatred, strife, oppression, and greed that we see are not according to thy will. Grant unto us courage to oppose evil and to do all in our power to bring in thy kingdom of love. In the seeming security of this moment may we put away selfishness, hatred, or other un-Christian attitudes which make for war. Give unto us a clearer vision of the meaning of brotherhood and lead us into victorious living. We ask, not for ourselves, but that thy will may be done, and thy kingdom come on earth. AMEN.

HYMN:

Forgive us, Christ, that through the years
    We call thee "Lord" in prayer,
Lift hymns of praise to thy dear name,
    Lay at thy feet each care;
While all our days thy clear commands
    We pass unheeding by,
Sing easily of brotherhood
    Which daily we deny.

Forgive us, we who talk of peace,
    While we re-arm for war,
Building anew our battle-lines
    In air, on sea, on shore.
Our prejudice of others' race
    No liturgy conceals;
How far removed from Christ's great love
    Our earthly way reveals.

Forgive that we who preach of light
    Live blind of others' need;
'Mid cries of those oppressed by want
    We still dispute our creed.
The cotton-cropper in the field,
    The worker in the mill,
The miner in the darkened shaft,
    When shall they know thy will?

Forgive us these our sins, dear Lord,
   But, oh, for this we pray,
That we may ne'er forgive our own
   Betrayal of thy way.
Arouse in us a hatred deep
   Of cowardice and greed,
That we may pledge ourselves anew
   To test our faith by deed.[5]

          —S. Ralph Harlow

BENEDICTION:

  May the love of God lead you into all truth. Amen.

SERVICE 31

GOD OF GRACE AND GOD OF GLORY

(Harry Emerson Fosdick)

AIM: To lead the group into a clearer conception of the challenge of the Christian religion.

PRELUDE: "Confidence" by Mendelssohn.

CALL TO WORSHIP:
> Holy, holy, holy, Lord God of Hosts,
> Heaven and earth are full of thy glory:
> Glory be to thee, O Lord, most high. AMEN.

HYMN: "Come, Thou, Almighty King," or
"The Voice of God Is Calling," or
"Glorious Things of Thee Are Spoken."

RESPONSIVE READING:

Leader: Our Lord Jesus Christ said: The first of all the commandments is, Hear, O Israel; the Lord our God is one Lord: and thou shalt love the Lord thy God with all thy heart, and with all thy soul, and with all thy mind, and with all thy strength. This is the first commandment.

Group: Lord, have mercy upon us, and incline our hearts to keep this law.

Leader: And the second is like, namely this, Thou shalt love thy neighbor as thyself.

Group: Lord, have mercy upon us, and incline our hearts to keep this law.

Leader: A new commandment I give unto you, That ye love one another; as I have loved you.

Group: Lord, have mercy upon us, and write all these laws in our hearts, we beseech thee. AMEN.[1]

POEM:

> All nature's works his praise declare,
> To whom they all belong;
> There is a voice in every star,
> In every breeze a song.
> Sweet music fills the world abroad
> With strains of love and power;
> The stormy sea sings praise to God,
> The thunder and the shower.
>
> To God the tribes of oceans cry,
> And birds upon the wing;
> To God the powers that dwell on high
> Their tuneful tribute bring.
> Like them, let man the throne surround,
> With them loud chorus raise,
> While instruments of loftier sound
> Assist his feeble praise.
>
> Great God, to thee we consecrate
> Our voices and our skill;
> We bid the pealing organ wait
> To speak alone thy will.
> Lord, while the music round us floats
> May earth-born passions die;
> O grant its rich and swelling notes
> May lift our souls on high!
> —HENRY WARE, JR.

HYMN: "A Mighty Fortress Is Our God."

STORY OF THE AUTHOR AND THE HYMN:

Harry Emerson Fosdick, pastor of Riverside Church of New York City, has made a place for himself in contemporary national history as few others among ministers have done in former generations. There are not many of the present day who share with him his prominence and popularity. It seems that in every generation one or more of God's gifted leaders take pre-eminence, and seemingly are set apart as mouthpieces for their generation. This privilege seems in this day to have been given to this eminent minister.[2]

Dr. Fosdick wrote the lines of this hymn for the dedication of the church on Riverside Drive over which he presides. It is a notable prayer addressed to the God of Grace and God of Glory. Like every true hymnist he belongs not to one denomination but to all, and he has expressed in the lines of this hymn a universal plea. This hymn has a message; and in order that our singing of it may have meaning and not be merely form, we must understand the message, and the purpose for which it was written.

Every line of this hymn is important; none of the stanzas should be omitted. The thought follows progressively and in order to get the message, the hymn must be used in its entirety. Dr. Fosdick has had opportunity to observe the trend of the times and with his ability to discern the needs of Christians today, he has written lines which are worthy of a place beside the utterances of the great leaders of the past. With rare insight he points out the significant ills of our generation and suggests a solution.

Dr. Fosdick's power of spiritual discernment has enabled him to diagnose the weaknesses which we deplore, the fears and doubts which too long have bound us. And in a fervent prayer in which Christians today will join heartily he prays to God to "cure thy children's warring madness, shame our wanton, selfish gladness, rich in things and poor in soul." He suggests a way out of our difficulties: wisdom and courage for the facing of this hour will come through prayer—by the pouring of God's power upon his children. As we sing this hymn, let us notice the steps by which we are to build the Kingdom of God.

RESPONSIVE READING:

Leader: Happy is the man that findeth wisdom, and the man that getteth understanding. She is more precious than rubies: and all the things thou canst desire are not to be compared unto her.

Group (to be sung):

> God of grace and God of glory,
> On thy people pour thy power;
> Crown thine ancient Church's story;
> Bring her bud to glorious flower.
> > Grant us wisdom,
> > Grant us courage,
> For the facing of this hour.

Leader: Blessed are the undefiled in the way, who walk in the law of the Lord. Blessed are they that keep his testimonies, and that seek him with the whole heart. Thy word have I hid in mine heart that I might not sin against thee.

Group: Lo! the hosts of evil round us
> Scorn thy Christ, assail his ways!
> Fears and doubts too long have bound us,
> Free our hearts to work and praise.
> > Grant us wisdom,
> > Grant us courage,
> For the living of these days.

Leader: Teach me, O Lord, the way of thy statutes, and I shall keep it unto the end. Give me understanding, and I shall keep thy law; yea, I shall observe it with my whole heart.

Group: Cure thy children's warring madness,
> Bend our pride to thy control;
> Shame our wanton, selfish gladness,
> Rich in things and poor in soul.
> > Grant us wisdom,
> > Grant us courage,
> Lest we miss thy kingdom's goal.

Leader: Trust in the Lord with all thine heart; and lean not unto thine own understanding. In all thy ways acknowledge him, and he shall direct thy paths.

Group: Set our feet on lofty places;
> Gird our lives that they may be
> Armored with all Christlike graces

In the fight to set men free.
  Grant us wisdom,
  Grant us courage,
That we fail not man nor thee!

Leader: I delight to do thy will, O my God: yea, thy law is within
my heart. I have not hid thy righteousness within my heart;
I have declared thy faithfulness and thy salvation: I have not
concealed thy lovingkindness and thy truth from the great
congregation.

Group: Save us from weak resignation
  To the evil we deplore;
Let the search for thy salvation
  Be our glory evermore.
    Grant us wisdom,
    Grant us courage,
Serving thee whom we adore.[3]

POEM:

Go, labor on! spend and be spent;
  Thy joy to do the Father's will:
It is the way the Master went—
  Should not the servant tread it still?

Go, labor on! 'tis not for naught,
  Thine earthly loss is heavenly gain;
Men heed thee, love thee, praise thee not;
  The Master praises—what are men?

Go, labor on, while it is day;
  The world's dark night is hastening on:
Speed, speed thy work, cast sloth away;
  It is not thus that souls are won.

Men die in darkness at your side,
  Without a hope to cheer the tomb:
Take up the torch, and wave it wide,
  The torch that lights time's thickest gloom.
                                   —HORATIUS BONAR

PRAYER:

Almighty God, our heavenly Father, thou who hast been our help in ages past, we come into thy presence with a keener appreciation of thy majesty. Grant that we may value more highly the heritage which has come to us, and help us to appreciate the privilege of carrying on the work which others have begun. Kindle in our hearts a faith that will not shrink before the challenge of today; give unto us courage to attack the evils which we deplore; and grant us wisdom for the living of these days. May ours be a steadfast faith which will make the coming of thy kingdom, not a future probability, but a present reality in our own lives. In the name of Christ, our Leader. AMEN.

BENEDICTION:

Now unto him who shall supply all your needs according to his riches in glory; unto God our Father be glory for ever and ever. AMEN.

SERVICE 32

SILENT NIGHT

(*Joseph Mohr—Franz Gruber*)

AIM: To lead the group into a fuller measure of peace and joy, and to a dedication of their lives to the Christ whose birthday they celebrate.

PRELUDE: Hymn tune "The First Noel."

CALL TO WORSHIP:

> O holy Child of Bethlehem!
> Descend to us, we pray;
> Cast out our sin, and enter in,
> Be born in us today!
> We hear the Christmas angels
> The great glad tidings tell;
> O come to us, abide with us,
> Our Lord Immanuel!
> —PHILLIPS BROOKS

HYMN: "O Little Town of Bethlehem," or
"Angels from the Realms of Glory."

SCRIPTURE:

And there were in the same country shepherds abiding in the field, keeping watch over their flock by night. And, lo, the angel of the Lord came upon them, and the glory of the Lord shone round about them: and they were sore afraid. And the angel said unto them, Fear not: for, behold, I bring you good tidings of great joy, which shall be to all people. For unto you is born this day, in the city of David, a Saviour, which is Christ the Lord. And this shall be a sign unto you: Ye shall find the babe wrapped in swaddling clothes, lying in a manger.

And suddenly there was with the angel a multitude of the heavenly host praising God, and saying, Glory to God in the highest, and on earth peace, good will toward men.

And it came to pass, as the angels were gone away from them into heaven, the shepherds said one to another, Let us now go even unto Bethlehem, and see this thing which is come to pass, which the Lord hath made known unto us. And they came with haste, and found Mary, and Joseph, and the babe lying in a manger.[1]

POEM:

> Long years ago o'er Bethlehem's hills
>   Was seen a wondrous thing;
> As shepherds watched their sleeping flocks
>   They heard the angels sing.
> The anthem rolled among the clouds
>   When earth was hushed and still;
> Its notes proclaimed sweet peace on earth
>   To all mankind good will.
>
> That song is sung by rich and poor,
>   Where'er the Christ is known;
> 'Tis sung in words, and sung in deeds,
>   Which bind all hearts in one.
> Angels are still the choiristers,
>   But we the shepherds are,
> To bear the message which they bring,
>   To those both near and far.
>   —LEIGH R. BREWER

PRAYER:

Our Father, we come into thy presence as simply, humbly, and reverently as did the shepherds of old to thank thee for the Christ whose birthday we celebrate. We are grateful for the gift of thy Son to the world, and for thy plan of salvation which is so great that it reaches us even today. Help us to become more worthy to

SILENT NIGHT

kneel with those who have worshiped thee through all the past ages. Give unto us the courage, faith, and loyalty of those who journeyed to Bethlehem to worship the Christ child. In Jesus' name. AMEN.

SPECIAL MUSIC: "Silent Night" (violin solo).

STORY OF THE AUTHOR AND THE HYMN:

The hymn "Silent Night," describing a scene tranquil and serene, was written hurriedly for an emergency. On the day before Christmas Eve, in the year 1818, Franz Gruber discovered that his organ was broken. A blizzard was raging outside. There was no chance of getting repairs from the neighboring village. Desperately he implored his friend, the priest Joesph Mohr, to write a hymn for the Christmas service, a hymn so simple that it could be sung without the organ.

Late in the evening the priest was called to administer the last rites to a dying woman. Returning he paused to look at the snow-capped peaks of the Austrian Alps, as they rose in grandeur above the peaceful little valley in the Tyrol. The blizzard was ended. Here and there a faint light glimmered in the village, and over all was that vast silence of Nature on a winter evening.

Suddenly it occurred to the priest that the night when Christ was born must have been like this. Powerfully affected, he hastened home and wrote the words which came into his mind. A strange peace and joy filled his heart as he read the stanzas again and again. Arising early the next morning, he took the manuscript to the organist and read it to him. As Franz Gruber listened to the lovely words, inner voices seemed to fill his humble quarters with an angelic chorus.

Catching the spirit of the hymn, Gruber began to set down the simple, flowing tune as it came to him. When it was finished, he sang it to his wife, who was tremendously moved. "We will die, you and I," she remarked, "but this song will live." Gruber's real contribution lies, however, in the beauty and simplicity of the tune, which is so unpretentious that it can be played with a few chords on a guitar.

On Christmas Eve the organ did not sound in the church at Arnsdorf. At first the congregation felt a lack of it, until, with Father Mohr singing, and Franz Gruber playing on his guitar, the hallowed strains of "Silent Night" fell upon their ears. They were deeply touched, though they did not realize that they were hearing the first rendition of one of the greatest Christmas hymns ever written.

— 207 —

The hymn came into fame slowly. For nearly a year it lay almost forgotten in Franz Gruber's desk. The following November the church organ was again in need of repair, and Gruber was asked to play something to test the organ. As the melody of "Silent Night" came back to him he struck the chords, and the workman was so entranced by the song that he begged for a copy to take to his village of Zillerthal across the mountains.

In this village the hymn became the favorite of four sisters by the name of Strasser, who were known for their well-trained voices. They sang the hymn in the great cathedrals of Leipzig; other wandering Tyrolese singers helped to start it on its way around the world. At that time it was without a name, and was known as "The Tyrolese Song," taking its name from the mountains from which it came.

Twenty-four years later the hymn was printed for the first time. When it was sung in the Imperial Church in Berlin, the Emperor was so enthusiastic that he ordered it be given first place in all religious Christmas programs. Since that time it has been translated into many languages and carried all over the world. Composed to be sung once, and in an emergency, by a humble village choir, this hymn has lived for more than a century.

There is careful progression in the thought of the hymn; the setting is given in a few words. We can picture the quietness of the night, with darkness everywhere except in the cave where the travelers are resting after their tiresome journey. Suddenly the light from heaven shows 'round about them, and a company of heavenly hosts begin singing "Alleluia," an anthem of praise directed to God in the highest. This is followed by the announcement, "Peace on earth, good will to men." The climax is reached in the prayer that the Star may guide us as we bring sincere adoration and praise into the presence of the King.[2]

HYMN: "Silent Night."

DIRECTED MEDITATION:

On one night, only, O Christ, may I light a candle in my wreath-hung window to welcome thee before the world. On only one day may I tie the flaunting crimson ribbons that help to make evident my joy at thy coming. The time for merrymaking is short and shining and sweet, and I thank thee for its loveliness. But I thank thee more that there is no hour in all the year when I may not make thee welcome in my heart. May I honor thee by keeping it aglow when no fragrance of pine boughs, no glory of giving, kindle it to remembrance. As I lose the red and green and gold of thy birthday may I but gain thee.[3]

As I watch the Christmas candles burn, I see in them a symbol of the Great Love which dipped a lustrous Spirit into human form that the world in its darkness might be illumined and made beautiful.[4]

Remain to me more beautiful, more beloved, more real than any of the romance that clusters around thy birthday.[4] AMEN.

HYMN: "There's a Song in the Air."

POEM:

> Upon the dim Judean hills,
>   The shepherds watched their flock by night,
> When on their unexpectant gaze
>   Outshone that vision of delight,
>   The fairest that did ever rise
>   To awe and gladden earthly eyes.
>
> From no far realm those shepherds came,
>   Treading the pilgrim's weary road;
> Not theirs the vigil and the fast
>   Within the hermit's mean abode;
>   'Twas at their usual task they stood,
>   When dawned that light of matchless good.
>
> Not only to the sage and seer
>   Life's revelation comes in grace;
> Most often on the toiler true,
>   Who, working steadfast in his place,
>   Looks for the coming of God's will,
>   The glorious vision shineth still.[5]
>   —EFFIE SMITH ELY

BENEDICTION:

Our Father, grant unto us in the fullest measure the peace and joy of the Christmas season, as we dedicate our lives to the Christ whose birthday we celebrate. AMEN.

SERVICE 33

AMERICA THE BEAUTIFUL

(*Katherine Lee Bates*)

AIM: To lead to a greater love of our country and to a desire to attain the ideals on which it was founded.

PRELUDE: Hymn tune "Austrian Hymn."

CALL TO WORSHIP:

I was glad when they said unto me, Let us go into the house of the Lord. Our feet shall stand within thy gates, O Jerusalem. Peace be within thy walls, and prosperity within thy palaces. Peace be within thee.

PRAYER HYMN:

My God, I thank thee, who hast made
  The earth so bright,
So full of splendor and of joy,
  Beauty and light;
So many glorious things are here,
  Noble and right.

I thank thee, too, that thou hast made
  Joy to abound;
So many gentle thoughts and deeds
  Circling us 'round,
That in the darkest spot of earth
  Some love is found.

I thank thee more that all our joy
    Is touched with pain,
That shadows fall on brightest hours,
    That thorns remain;
So that earth's bliss may be our guide,
    And not our chain.

I thank thee, Lord, that thou hast kept
    The best in store;
We have enough, yet not too much,
    To long for more;
A learning for a deeper peace
    Not known before. AMEN.[1]
           —ADELAIDE A. PROCTER

SCRIPTURE:

For, lo, he that formeth the mountains, and created the wind,
And declared unto man what is his thought;
That maketh the morning darkness, and treadeth upon the high
    places of the earth—
The Lord, the God of Hosts, is his name.

Seek him that maketh the Pleiades and Orion,
And turneth the shadow of death into the morning,
And maketh the day dark with night;
That calleth for the waters of the sea,
And poureth them out upon the face of the earth—
The Lord is his name.

Thine, O Lord, is the greatness, and the power,
And the glory, and the victory; and the majesty:
For all that is in the heaven and in the earth is thine;
Thine is the kingdom, O Lord,
And thou art exalted as head above all.
All things come of thee,
And of thine own have we given thee.[2]

HYMN: "O God, Beneath Thy Guiding Hand," or
      "God of Our Fathers, Whose Almighty Hand."

POEM:

Not for our lands, our wide-flung prairie wealth,
   Our mighty rivers born of friendly spring.
Our inland seas, our mountains proud and high,
   Forests and orchards richly blossoming;
Not for these, Lord, our deepest thanks are said
   As, humbly glad, we hail this day serene;
Not for these most, dear Father of our lives,
   But for the love that in all things is seen.

We thank thee not for prestige born of war,
   For dauntless navies built for battle stress;
Now would we boast of armies massed for strife;
   These all are vain, O Lord of kindliness.
What need have we of swords and bayonets,
   Of mighty cannon belching poisoned flame!
O, woo us from the pagan love of these
   Lest we again defile thy sacred name.

We thank thee, Lord, on this recurring day,
   For liberty to worship as we will;
We thank thee for the hero souls of old
   Who dared wild seas their mission to fulfill.
O, gird our hearts with stalwart faith in good,
   Give us new trust in thy providing hand,
And may a spirit born of brotherhood
   Inspire our hearts and bless our native land.[3]

            —THOMAS CURTIS CLARK

INTERPRETATION OF THE HYMN:

   The hymn "America the Beautiful" was inspired by a tour which Miss Katherine Lee Bates, the author, made of the United States. During the summer of 1893, while she was professor of English at Wellesley, she traveled from the east across the country to Colorado Springs, where she taught in the new summer school held in that resort. With a group of eastern professors she visited the Chicago World's Fair and was impressed by the beauty of the white buildings which she at once named "alabaster cities." But the climax of the tour came when she reached the Rockies and made the trip to the summit of Pike's Peak. The view of the "purple mountain majesties above the fruited plain" brought the inspiration for the lines of the hymn.

At that time there was no thought of sharing the poem; but two years later Miss Bates sent it to the *Congregationalist,* in which periodical it appeared in print for the first time. The poem attracted wide attention from the beginning and has steadily increased in popularity. It was set to music by an eminent composer, Silas G. Pratt, and was published in his *Famous Songs.* Since that time it has been sung to many tunes and has appeared in the leading hymnals of this country.

Not only is this hymn a favorite in America but in other countries as well. It has gone into Australia, where the young people use it in their meetings, substituting the name Australia for America; into Canada, where it is sung with the refrain, "O Canada"; and into Mexico, where the refrain, "Mi Mexico," is used. It is especially suitable for flag raisings and for other patriotic mass meetings. When asked about the popularity of the hymn, Miss Bates remarked, "That the hymn has gained, in these years, such a hold as it has upon our people, is clearly due to the fact that Americans are at heart idealists, with a fundamental faith in human brotherhood."

This is the most beautiful of our patriotic hymns. It reminds us of our noble past, of the Pilgrims who made a thoroughfare for freedom across the wilderness of this vast country. This thought is united with the vision of the great future of our country, which vision we shall attain if we hold fast to our ideal of brotherhood. Miss Bates emphasizes the fact that America cannot make these dreams come true and take her place among the nations of the world without the guidance of God and a strong determination to follow his purpose. She looks beyond the temporal beauty of man-made cities to the permanent "alabaster cities which shall be undimmed by human tears." Let us notice how the thought follows progressively in the lines of the hymn, and that each stanza closes with the prayer that God lend his aid as we strive to hold on to our high ideals and attain our real destiny among the nations.

LITANY:

Leader: Blessed is the nation whose God is the Lord; and the people whom he hath chosen for his own inheritance. Righteousness exalteth a nation; but sin is a reproach to any people.

Group: (to be sung)

> O beautiful for spacious skies,
>> For amber waves of grain,
> For purple mountain majesties
>> Above the fruited plain!
> America! America!
>> God shed his grace on thee,
> And crown thy good with brotherhood
>> From sea to shining sea.

Leader: Proclaim liberty throughout the land unto all the inhabitants thereof. Loose the bands of wickedness, and undo the heavy burdens. Let the oppressed go free. Break every yoke!

Group:

> O beautiful for pilgrim feet,
>> Whose stern, impassioned stress
> A thoroughfare for freedom beat
>> Across the wilderness!
> America! America!
>> God mend thine every flaw,
> Confirm thy soul in self-control,
>> Thy liberty in law.

Leader: Open ye the gates, that the righteous nation which keepeth the truth may enter in.

Group:

> O beautiful for heroes proved
>> In liberating strife,
> Who more than self their country loved,
>> And mercy more than life!
> America! America!
>> May God thy gold refine,
> Till all success be nobleness,
>> And every gain divine.

Leader: God hath made of one blood all nations of men, for to dwell on all the face of the earth; therefore nation shall not lift up a sword against nation, neither shall they learn war any more.[4]

Group:

> O beautiful for patriot dream
>> That sees, beyond the years,
> Thine alabaster cities gleam,
>> Undimmed by human tears!

America! America!
　God shed his grace on thee,
And thy good with brotherhood
　From sea to shining sea.

POEM:

More famed than Rome, as splendid as old Greece,
And saintlier than Hebrew prophet's dream . . . .

In thoughts, as wise as is her prairie sea;
In deeds, as splendid as her mountain piles;
As noble as her mighty rivers tides.
Let her be true, a land where right abides;
Let her be clean, as sweet as summer isles;
And let her sound the note of liberty
For all the earth, till every man and child be free! [5]
　　　　　　　　—THOMAS CURTIS CLARK

UNISON PRAYER:

Creator and Ruler of mankind, we pray thee this day for our country, that her new life may be established and built up in thyself; that all hatred and malice, all indifference to the suffering of others, all narrow exclusiveness and selfish greed, may be swept away by the breath of thy Spirit; and that public spirit, honor, and justice, co-operation in service, self-sacrifice for the good of the whole people may flourish abundantly among us. We pray thee also for ourselves, that thou wilt forge us into tools meet for the service of our country; burn from us all selfishness and pride, purify us from all baseness, fill us with thy divine passion to uplift the weak, to sweep away oppression and wrong, to give to every man, even to the lowest and most degraded, the opportunity for a full life that may be lived to thy glory and to the service of mankind. In Jesus' name we pray. AMEN.[6]

HYMN: "The Land We Love Is Calling," or
　　　"My Country, 'Tis of Thee."

BENEDICTION:

May the God of peace be with us as we go forth to spread the reign of righteousness. AMEN.

CHRIST THE LORD IS RISEN TODAY

(Charles Wesley)

AIM: To lead to a clearer conception of the meaning of the resurrection.

PRELUDE: Hymn tune "Easter Hymn."

CALL TO WORSHIP:

Leader: Lift up your heads, ye mighty gates,
Behold, the King of glory waits;
The King of kings is drawing near;
The Saviour of the world is here!

Fling wide the portals of your heart;
Make it a temple, set apart
From earthly use for Heaven's employ,
Adorned with prayer, and love, and joy.

Group: Redeemer, come, we open wide
Our hearts to thee; here, Lord, abide.
Thine inner presence let us feel;
Thy grace and love in us reveal.

—GEORG WEISSEL

HYMN: "Rejoice the Lord Is King," or
"All Hail the Power of Jesus' Name."

CHRIST THE LORD IS RISEN TODAY

O thou Christ Immortal, who by thy victory over death hast brought life and immortality to light; raise us, by faith in thee, from the grave of sin, and deliver us from the moral darkness of disbelief: that our hearts may be fortified with an eternal hope, and our affections set upon the things which are above. In Jesus' name. AMEN.[1]

SCRIPTURE:

In the end of the sabbath, as it began to dawn toward the first day of the week, came Mary Magdalene, and the other Mary, to see the sepulchre. And, behold, there was a great earthquake: for the angel of the Lord descended from heaven, and came and rolled back the stone from the door, and sat upon it. His countenance was like lightning, and his raiment white as snow: and for fear of him the keepers did shake, and became as dead men. And the angel answered and said unto the women, Fear not ye: for I know that ye seek Jesus, which was crucified. He is not here; for he is risen, as he said. Come, see the place where the Lord lay. And go quickly, and tell his disciples that he is risen from the dead; and, behold, he goeth before you into Galilee; there shall ye see him: lo, I have told you. And they departed quickly from the sepulchre, with fear and great joy, and did run to bring his disciples word.[2]

POEM:

Sing, soul of mine, this day of days.
  The Lord is risen.
Toward the sunrising set thy face.
  The Lord is risen.
Behold he giveth strength and grace;
For darkness, light; for morning, praise;
For sin, his holiness; for conflict, peace.
Arise, O soul, this Easter Day!
Forget the tomb of yesterday,
For thou from bondage art set free;
Thou sharest in his victory,
And life eternal is for thee,
Because the Lord is risen.
                    —AUTHOR UNKNOWN

INTERPRETATION:

During the same year that Isaac Watts brought out his "Hymns and Spiritual Songs," there was born to Samuel and Susannah Wesley, in the Epworth parsonage, a son who was destined to carry on the work of Watts. This son Charles and his brother John were nicknamed "Methodists" while they were students at Christ's Church, Oxford, because of the strict rules which they imposed upon themselves. This name was given later to the denomination which came into existence as a result of their labors.

The more famous brother, John, was occupied with preaching and organizing the societies, while Charles made his contribution largely through hymn writing. As these brothers traveled over the country, they sought out the laborers, farmers, and miners who had been uninfluenced by the dignified and stately services of the Church of England. At first they ministered to the lower and middle classes, but gradually the upper classes were also reached. Revivals sprang up all over England and spread to America. The hymns had a far-reaching influence, for they touched many that the sermons left unmoved. It was through the singing of the hymns that the unchurched masses found a means of expressing their new-found joy in Christianity and were gradually lifted to higher levels of living.

Charles was a different type of person from his brother John. He was a man of poetic moods, and verses came to him at all times—while on horseback, in the stagecoach, or walking. So full of enthusiasm was he that his hymn writing became almost a passion with him. He wrote about every type of experience and every stage of development in the life of a Christian. He wrote more than sixty-five hundred hymns, many of which are still in use today.

When we wish to lift our hearts in Easter praise, we use Charles Wesley's beautiful song of the Resurrection, "Christ the Lord Is Risen Today." The glad "Alleluia" at the end of each line is most appropriate for Easter. From the earliest time the Christians saluted each other on Easter morning with "Alleulia, the Lord is risen," and the response was "He is risen indeed." The word "Alleluia" comes from two Hebrew words and is sometimes translated, "Praise ye the Lord: The Lord's name be praised."

Jerome, writing in the fourth century, tells us that Christian plowmen shouted "Alleluia" while at their work. Other writers record the fact that sailors used the term as a shout of encouragement while plying their oars. Among all of the festivals of the year, certainly Easter is one of the most appropriate for singing praise to God.[3]

Easter has always been one of the outstanding festivals in the Greek Church. In Athens a solemn service is held in the church on the evening before Easter. Following the service, as the midnight hour approaches, the archbishop and his priests and the king and queen leave the church and take their places upon a raised platform outside. Thousands of people with unlighted tapers gather around the platform as the priests chant softly. When the sound of cannon announces the hour of midnight, the archbishop raises the cross and exclaims joyously, "Christ is risen"; this is echoed and re-echoed while a burst of light speeds through the crowd from the lighted tapers. Men clasp each other's hands and rejoice as if some great joy had suddenly come to them. Bands play and rockets answer from neighboring hills while many voices are raised in praise to God.

The message of Easter is found in the first line of this hymn, and through its entirety there is expressed praise for the continued presence of the ever-living Christ. The author is attempting to bring to us a recognition of the power of the resurrection. He would have us realize that not only is there victory over death, but a greater miracle is wrought in the transforming power which Christ brings into our lives. When the unseen Christ becomes a reality to us, and we act as though we are living in his presence, a new power comes to us which will enable us to live the trimphant life.

HYMN:

> Christ the Lord is risen today,
> > Alleluia!
> Sons of men and angels say,
> > Alleluia!
> Raise your joys and triumphs high,
> > Alleluia!
> Sing, ye heavens, and earth reply,
> > Alleluia!
>
> Lives again our glorious King,
> > Alleluia!
> Where, O death, is now thy sting?
> > Alleluia!

Once he died, our souls to save,
    Alleluia!
Where's thy victory, boasting grave?
    Alleluia!

Love's redeeming work is done,
    Alleluia!
Fought the fight, the battle won,
    Alleluia!
Death in vain forbids him rise,
    Alleluia!
Christ hath opened Paradise,
    Alleluia!

Soar we now where Christ has led,
    Alleluia!
Following our exalted Head,
    Alleluia!
Made like him, like him we rise,
    Alleluia!
Ours the cross, the grave, the skies,
    Alleluia!

          —CHARLES WESLEY

POEM:

Life gleams anew in the freshened grasses
  On each bare slope;
Shall not the sere fields of the spirit
  Shine glad with hope?

Thrush and bluebird to hill and forest
  Their music bring;
Have human lips in this sacred dawning
  No cause to sing?

Seeds that the farmer sowed are sprouting
  From furrows deep;
Shall glorious lives remain forever
  In winter sleep?

Since One arose on Easter morning
  In a new tomb laid,
I face the gloom of life's decaying
  All unafraid;

For surely as leaves on trees are greening
  In springtime's breath,
I know that our souls shall rise up fadeless
  From frosts of death! [4]

—EFFIE SMITH ELY

LITANY OF PRAISE:

Leader: Our Father, for the gift of thy Son to mankind

Group: Accept our thanks, we pray.

Leader: For his death upon the cross and for the example of his life

Group: We give thee thanks, O Lord.

Leader: For the joy of Easter and the hope of new life which it brings

Group: We give thee thanks, O Lord.

Leader: For the gift of thy Holy Spirit

Group: We give thee thanks, O Lord.

Leader: For every impulse to follow the way of the cross

Group: We give thee thanks, O Lord.

Leader: Come into our lives and help us to triumph over all sin.

Group: In Jesus' Name. AMEN.

BENEDICTION:

Grant that the miracle of thy transforming power may be wrought in our lives. AMEN.

SERVICE 35

MARCHING WITH THE HEROES
(*William George Tarrant*)

AIM: To lead to a new insight of the meaning of heroic living.

PRELUDE: Hymn Tune "Godfrey."

CALL TO WORSHIP:

> Sing to the Lord a joyful song,
>   Lift up your hearts, your voices raise;
> To us his gracious gifts belong,
>   To him our songs of love and praise.
>
> For life and love, for rest and food,
>   For daily help and nightly care,
> Sing to the Lord, for he is good,
>   And praise his name, for it is fair.
>   —JOHN S. B. MONSELL

HYMN: "Dare to Be Brave, Dare to be True," or
"March On, O Soul, with Strength."

RESPONSIVE READING:

Leader: Be strong and of a good courage, fear not: for the Lord thy God, he it is that doth go with thee; he will not fail thee, nor forsake thee.

Group: The Lord is my strength and my shield: my heart trusted in him and I am helped; therefore my heart greatly rejoiceth, and with song will I praise him.

Leader: Watch ye, stand fast in the faith, quit you like men, be strong.

MARCHING WITH THE HEROES

Group: The Lord God will help me; the Lord is my strength and song, and is become my salvation.

Leader: Even the youths shall faint and be weary, and the young men shall utterly fail: but they that wait for the Lord shall renew their strength; they shall mount up with wings as eagles; they shall run, and not be weary, and they shall walk, and not faint.

Group: Therefore, will we be strong and of good courage: The Lord of hosts is with us: Blessed be his holy name.[1]

PRAYER:

> Talk with us, Lord, thyself reveal,
>   While here o'er earth we rove;
> Speak to our hearts, and let us feel
>   The kindling of thy love.
>
> With thee conversing, we forget
>   All time, and toil, and care;
> Labor is rest, and pain is sweet,
>   If thou, my God, art here.
>
> Here then, my God, vouchsafe to stay,
>   And bid my heart rejoice;
> My bounding heart shall own thy sway,
>   And echo to thy voice.
>
> Let this my every hour employ,
>   Till I thy glory see;
> Enter into my Master's joy,
>   And find my heaven in thee. AMEN.
>   —CHARLES WESLEY

PRAYER RESPONSE:

> Hear our prayer, O Lord,
> Hear our prayer, O Lord,
> Incline thine ear to us,
> And grant us thy peace. AMEN.

SCRIPTURE:

And what shall I more say? for the time would fail me to tell of Gideon, and of Barak, and of Samson, and of Jephthah; of David also, and Samuel, and of the prophets; who through faith subdued kingdoms, wrought righteousness, obtained promises, stopped the mouths of lions, quenched the violence of fire, escaped the edge of the sword, out of weakness were made strong, waxed valiant in fight, turned to flight the armies of the aliens. Women received their dead raised to life again: and others were tortured, not accepting deliverance; that they might obtain a better resurrection: and others had a trial of cruel mockings and scourgings, yea, moreover, of bonds and imprisonment: they were stoned, they were sawn asunder, were tempted, were slain with the sword: they wandered about in sheepskins and goatskins; being destitute, afflicted, tormented (of whom the world was not worthy); they wandered in deserts, and in mountains, and in dens and caves of the earth. And these all, having obtained a good report through faith, received not the promise: God having provided some better thing for us, that they without us should not be made perfect.[2]

STORY:

On an elevation far back from the busy streets of a city stood a massive building whose architecture suggested a Grecian temple. Above the building the dome seemed to reach the very clouds. There was a wide entrance, approached by a long flight of steps, at the top of which stood a man.

"Will you tell me what this building is?" I inquired.

"This is the Hall of Heroes. Would you like to see the interior?" replied the guide.

Following him, I found myself in the center of a spacious hall, lighted with the afternoon sun as it filtered through the stained-glass windows. When my guide spoke, his voice echoed along the walls like the notes of a cathedral organ. "Here we enshrine," said he, "the memories of all heroes. Many famous ones are here, but there are others who are unknown outside their own neighborhood. We welcome the least along with the greatest."

There was a large book in the center of the room and when I asked about it, the guide said, "That is the Book of Life. Would you like to see your page?"

"Oh, no," I hastened to reply, "I do not care to see the record of my deeds."

"Come, you must see the building." The guide led me to the stairs over which were written the words, "How glorious it is to die for one's country!" Over the door in letters of gold I read, "Heroes of War." As I walked along the aisles I saw many familiar names: Leonidas who fell at Thermopylae, Horatius at the bridge, Nelson with his armless sleeve, Gordon without a weapon, Washington, and Robert E. Lee. Thinking of the sacrifice of so many men, my guide said, "Some day the nations of the world will learn to live together as neighbors, loving one another as children of one Father. Let us go to the next floor."

Mounting the stairs, I saw these words inscribed, "There is a path that the eye of the eagle hath not seen," and over the door were carved the words, "Heroes of the Lonely Way." "In this room," continued the guide, "are the pioneers of all ages who have pushed their way through the wilderness to settle new country. They have scaled mountain heights, crossed deserts, sailed unknown oceans, and charted strange places. Here are adventurers, such as Columbus, Magellan, Balboa, LaSalle, and others whose discoveries have meant more to the world than all the conquests of the sword."

I would have lingered in this room, but my guide led me to the next floor. Over an open door I read the inscription, "Heroes of Truth." Among the vast throng who had stood for the truth, the guide pointed out Socrates with the cup of hemlock in his hand, Stephen suffering martyrdom, Martin Luther nailing the thesis on the door of the church, and Pasteur with his test tubes. The room fascinated me, but the guide led me to another flight of stairs over which were the words, "Greater love hath no man than this, that a man lay down his life for his friends." He stood aside that I might read the words over the door, "Heroes of Love."

I realized that we were now in the dome of the building. At first the light was of such brilliance that I could not distinguish the figures. After a time I saw a young child in his mother's arms; then, I saw a strong young man with clear eyes and thoughtful brow. He it was who taught the multitude, healed the sick, brought sight to the blind and comfort to the sorrowing. Finally I saw him as he hung upon the cross.

Growing accustomed to the light, I realized that this room was the fullest of all, for the walls, stretching away in the distance, left no space unfilled. I began to distinguish faces—there were Livingstone, Lincoln, John G. Paton, Judson, Florence Nightingale, Edith Cavell, and countless others. I was irresistibly drawn to the figure of Christ. Standing there with my eyes fastened upon the Hero of all heroes, I caught a distant strain of music, growing louder and louder, until it filled the entire building. The familiar hymn "Marching with the Heroes" was being sung, and it was coming from every floor of the building.

I felt that I could stand it no longer; so I fled from the room with the music still ringing in my ears. When I stopped, my guide at my side said in a calm voice, "You will be in our building some day."

"I, a hero?" I stammered.

"Why not?" he asked.

As I looked into his eyes I saw that his face bore a strange resemblance to the face of Christ. He inquired, "On which floor would you like for us to prepare a room for you?"

Before I could reply the vision had vanished. What would you have said? [3]

HYMN:

Marching with the heroes,
 Comrades of the strong,
Lift we hearts and voices
 As we march along;
Oh, the joyful music
 All in chorus raise!
Theirs the song of triumph,
 Ours the song of praise.

Glory to the heroes,
 Who, in days of old,
Trod the path of duty,
 Faithful, wise, and bold;
For the right unflinching,
 Strong the weak to save,
Warriors all and freemen,
 Fighting for the slave.

So we sing the story
  Of the brave and true,
Till among the heroes
  We are heroes, too;
Loyal to our Captain,
  Like the men of yore,
Marching with the heroes,
  Onward, evermore.[4]
　　　　—WILLIAM GEORGE TARRANT

LITANY OF SUPPLICATION:

Leader: O God, our Father, for the records of the deeds of the great men of all ages,

Group: We give thee thanks.

Leader: For the teachings of Jesus and the example of a perfect life,

Group: We give thee thanks.

Leader: In the strength of our youth, give us the courage to follow the example of Jesus,

Group: We beseech thee, O Lord.

Leader: In the midst of much confusion concerning the right, help us to know the true from the false, the good from the evil,

Group: We beseech thee, O Lord.

Leader: When evil is made alluring, give us the strength to resist temptation,

Group: We beseech thee, O Lord.

Leader: In this age of freedom, give unto us the wisdom to make right choices.

Group: We beseech thee, O Lord.

Leader: Now in the days of our youth, give unto us a portion of thy Spirit, and lead us into larger fields of usefulness.

Group: In Jesus' name. AMEN.

BENEDICTION:

Keep us as thine own, O God, and fill our hearts with thy love through Christ, the Hero of all heroes. AMEN.

SERVICE 36

I WOULD BE TRUE

(Howard Arnold Walter)

AIM: To help the group to come to a decision to live according to the highest and best they know.

PRELUDE: "Largo Appassionato" by Beethoven.

CALL TO WORSHIP:

> The earth is hushed in silence,
> Its cares now flee away;
> Let all things bow in reverence
> On this the Lord's own day.
>
> The bells are sweetly ringing,
> Their clear-toned voices say:
> "Ye people, come and worship
> On this the Lord's own day."
>
> Come, all ye thankful people:
> Why should our hearts delay
> To greet the Lord of heaven
> On this his holy day?
> —ANONYMOUS

HYMN: "Now in the Days of Youth," or
"My Soul, Be on Thy Guard."

I WOULD BE TRUE

UNISON PRAYER:

Almighty Lord, with one accord,
   We offer thee our youth,
And pray that thou would'st give us now
   The warfare of the truth.

Thy cause doth claim our souls by name,
   Because that we are strong;
In all the land, one steadfast band,
   May we to Christ belong.

Let fall on every college hall
   The luster of thy cross,
That love may dare thy work to share
   And count all else but loss.

Our hearts be ruled, our spirits schooled
   Alone thy will to seek,
And when we find thy blessed mind,
   Instruct our lips to speak. AMEN.
           —M. WOOLSEY STRYKER

LITANY:

Leader: Seeing we are compassed about with so great a cloud of witnesses, let us lay aside every weight, and the sin which doth so easily beset us, and let us run with patience the race that is set before us, looking unto Jesus the author and finisher of our faith.

Group: Thou, whose feet once trod the way
   Trod by us in work and play,
   Through the hours of school today
      Shield and save us!

Leader: Let your light so shine before men, that they may see your good works, and glorify your Father which is in heaven.

Group: From a life by pride accursed,
   Loveless craving to be first,
   Hearts that scorn thy least and worst,
      Shield and save us!

Leader: Whatsoever ye would that men should do to you, do ye even
so to them.

Group: By the love that stooped to earth,
By thy gracious human birth,
By thy childhood's tears and mirth,
Shield and save us!

Leader: Seek ye first the kingdom of God, and his righteousness; and
all these things shall be added unto you.

Group: Till the school of life is o'er,
Said the tasks and shut the door,
Jesus, now and evermore,
Shield and save us! AMEN.[1]

DIRECTED MEDITATION:

Let us think of Jesus in the days of his flesh. . . . At our age what
longings, desires, and temptations did he have? . . . What were his
deals? . . . What self-imposed standards did he set up for himself? . . .
Were any of his problems similiar to ours? . . . What does he expect
of each one of us today? . . . Are all of our standards entirely
Christian? . . . What changes would I have to make in my life if
I came up to the standard that Jesus expects of each one of us?

HYMN:

Young and radiant, he is standing
As he stood at Salem's shrine;
Just a lad forever,
With a look and grace divine!
"Tell me, how it is ye sought me?
Wist ye not my Father's plan?
I must be about his business,
Would I be a Son of Man."

I can see him humbly kneeling,
As he knelt upon the hill;
While the waters hushed their music,
And the night grew bright and still:
"Brothers, tell me why ye sought me?
Wist ye not my Father's plan?

— 230 —

I WOULD BE TRUE

He must grow in grace and wisdom,
  Who would be a Son of Man."

Like a flame his soul is striking
  In his wrath at greed and shame;
"Ye have made a den of robbers
  Of the temple to his name;
Know ye not his equal justice?
  Wist ye not my Father's plan?
He must bathe his sword in heaven
  Who would be a Son of Man."

I can see him dying, loving
  Unto death on Calvary;
His dear hands still pleading, praying,
  Worn and torn for you and me!
"Brothers, will ye scorn and leave me?
  Wist ye not my Father's plan?
He must wear a crown of sorrow
  Who would be a Son of Man." [2]

—ALLEN EASTMAN CROSS

SCRIPTURE:

Whatsoever things are true, whatsoever things are honest, whatsoever things are just, whatsoever things are pure, whatsoever things
are lovely, whatsoever things are of good report; if there be any virtue,
and if there be any praise, think on these things.[3]

STORY OF THE AUTHOR AND THE HYMN:

In two short stanzas of the hymn "I Would Be True" Howard
Arnold Walter has stated his life's purpose or creed. Coming out of his
own experience at a time when he was deciding upon his ideals and
standards, the hymn has struck a responsive chord in the hearts of
young people everywhere. He has caught the spirit of youth; in every
line there is high idealism and a challenge to courageous living. In
the hymn he has given a pattern which he himself followed in the
brief span of his life.

Mr. Walter was only twenty-three years old when he wrote the
lines of the hymn "I Would Be True" and did not intend that they

should be used as a hymn. He enclosed them in a letter as a personal message to his mother; and she, recognizing their beauty, sent them to *Harper's Magazine,* where they appeared in print for the first time under the title "My Creed." Later they found their way into many hymnbooks and became a favorite with young people everywhere.

Born in New Britain, Connecticut, in 1883, Mr. Walter graduated from Princeton in 1905 and later entered Hartford to prepare for the ministry. Following this training he taught English at Waseda University in Tokyo, Japan. It was here he wrote the hymn "I Would Be True." After one year in the Orient he returned to Hartford for further study. There many honors came to him, among them a fellowship which enabled him to study in Edinburgh and in Germany.

Mr. Walter spent two years in the ministry in America; but, his greatest interest being in the Orient, he again volunteered for foreign service. On account of a weak heart he could not pass the physical examination. Being advised by a physician that he had only a few years to live, he replied, "That makes it all the more essential that I get back to work at once." Failing to secure an appointment as a minister, he appealed to Dr. John R. Mott for a chance to serve abroad, and was sent as literary secretary for the Young Men's Christian Association at Lahore, India.

Mr. Walter's work in Lahore among the students in the Forman Christian College is outstanding. Besides his class work he gave his services untiringly as a counselor. At the time of his greatest usefulness he lost his life in the November, 1918, influenza epidemic which swept over the country. Hartford Seminary has placed his name on its honor roll, and a memorial tablet was erected in his home church in New Britain; but his most enduring monument is his hymn, which conveys a living, vital message to young people today.

The hymn was written in such a manner that there is no doubt concerning the message which the author wished to convey. The meaning is so clear and the truth so evident that there is little need for interpretation. The creed of his life is reflected in every line of the hymn. He was not an ascetic who withdrew from the world, neither was he a mystic who pondered over abstract questions, but instead he put his ideals to work in his everyday life. He gloried in strength and daring, not for himself, but for those who were weak and dependent upon him. He determined to hold on to his ideals, not for selfish reasons, but because there were those who would be hurt if he failed.

I WOULD BE TRUE

We are grateful for the legacy which Mr. Walter left to us in the message of this hymn.

HYMN:

> I would be true, for there are those who trust me;
> I would be pure, for there are those who care;
> I would be strong, for there is much to suffer;
> I would be brave, for there is much to dare.
>
> I would be friend of all, the foe, the friendless;
> I would be giving, and forget the gift;
> I would be humble, for I know my weakness;
> I would look up, and laugh, and love, and lift.
> —HOWARD ARNOLD WALTER

PRAYER:

O God, our Father, we thank thee for all the gifts which come from thee—for the truth which thou hast revealed, for the friends that we enjoy. Help us to become more worthy of our friendships. Grant that we may never disappoint our friends, but ever remain faithful to the trust which they have in us. Forgive us for the times when we have failed to live up to our ideals. Help us to choose high standards, and give us the power and the determination to live according to the best we know. For Jesus' sake. AMEN.

HYMN: "Are Ye Able?"

BENEDICTION:

Lead us in the paths of righteousness for Thy name's sake. AMEN.

SERVICE 37

THIS IS MY FATHER'S WORLD
(Maltbie D. Babcock)

AIM: To help the group to find a revelation of God through the beauty of nature.

PRELUDE: Hymn tune "Mercy." [1]

HYMN:

> Now, on land and sea descending,
>   Brings the night its peace profound;
> Let our vesper hymn be blending
>   With the holy calm around.
> Jubilate! Jubilate!
>   Jubilate! Amen!
>
> Soon as dies the sunset glory,
>   Stars of heaven shine out above,
> Telling still the ancient story—
>   Their Creator's changeless love.
>
> Now, our wants and burdens leaving
>   To his care who cares for all,
> Cease we fearing, cease we grieving:
>   At his touch our burdens fall.
>
> As the darkness deepens o'er us,
>   Lo! eternal stars arise;

THIS IS MY FATHER'S WORLD

Hope and faith and love rise glorious,
Shining in the spirit's skies.[2]
—SAMUEL LONGFELLOW

PRAYER:

Our Father, thou who art the Creator of all things, help us to be alive to all forms of beauty—of thought, word, or deed. Help us to see thy thoughtful care of us reflected in the beauty of the sunrise and the sunset, in the unfolding flower, in the loveliness of the springtime, in the splendor of the stars, and even in the grass under our feet. Grant that we may learn from nature to build into our own lives the same beauty and orderliness. May the peace and harmony of the out-of-doors calm our troubled spirits. In the name of the Master. AMEN.

PRAYER RESPONSE:

Hear our prayer, O Lord,
Hear our prayer, O Lord;
Incline thine ear to us,
And grant us thy peace. AMEN.

UNISON SCRIPTURE READING:

When I consider thy heavens, the work of thy fingers,
The moon and the stars, which thou hast ordained;
What is man, that thou art mindful of him?
And the son of man, that thou visitest him?
For thou hast made him a little lower than the angels,
And hast crowned him with glory and honor.
Thou madest him to have dominion over the works of thy hands;
Thou hast put all things under his feet:
All sheep and oxen, yea, and the beasts of the field;
The fowl of the air, and the fish of the sea,
And whatsoever passeth through the paths of the seas.
O Lord our Lord, how excellent is thy name in all the earth! [3]

HYMN: "Fairest, Lord Jesus," or
"For the Beauty of the Earth"

Poem:

I saw God wash the world last night
  With his sweet shower on high;
And then when morning came
  I saw him hang it out to dry.

He washed each tiny blade of grass,
  And every trembling tree;
He flung his shadows against the hills
  And swept the billowy sea.

The white rose is a cleaner white,
  The red rose is more red,
Since God washed every fragrant face
  And put them all to bed.

There's not a bird, there's not a bee,
  That wings along the way,
But is a cleaner bird and bee
  Than it was yesterday.

I saw God wash the world last night;
  Ah, would he had washed me
As clean of all my dust and dirt
  As that old white birch tree! [4]
        —William L. Stidger

Special Music: "Trees" (Joyce Kilmer).

Story of the Author and the Hymn:

The hymn "This Is My Father's World" was written by a minister, Dr. Maltbie D. Babcock. While in college he was a leader in athletics, being an expert swimmer and a star baseball pitcher. In every respect he was a splendid example of sturdy manhood. Few people have enjoyed the out-of-doors as he did. Although his pastorates were all in the city, he never lost an opportunity to go to the country, where he reveled in the beauty of mountains, skies, forests, and sea. There was a deep ravine about two miles from Lake Ontario in which many varieties of birds were to be seen. It was probably on one of his visits to this sanctuary that the lines of this hymn came to him.

THIS IS MY FATHER'S WORLD

Music came to Dr. Babcock so naturally that not only was he able to play several instruments with very little instruction but he also composed music. On one occasion an entire recital was given of his original compositions. He followed the gifted writer, Dr. Henry van Dyke, as pastor of the Brick Presbyterian Church in New York City, and remained there until his death.

The beauty of nature brought to Dr. Babcock not only joy, but a revelation of God himself. He thought of God as the Creator, and also as a loving heavenly Father whose presence is about us at all times, and who would have us enjoy the beauties of nature which he has created. Dr. Babcock saw God in the beauty of the lily, in the song of the birds, in the rustling grass. In fact, God spoke to him everywhere, in field, in forest, and in stream. In the second stanza of the hymn he states his idea of God so simply that even a child can understand.

The author strikes a new note in the third stanza. Praising God and reveling in the beauty about us is not all of life. The peace and harmony of nature make us feel that evil in the world should be corrected. Can we truly say, "This is my Father's world," until we have tried to make the world as it should be? The author expresses the idea that religion is not something to be enjoyed in a passive way, but that it should be an active force against evil. Though the wrong seems deeply intrenched, God is the ruler yet, and something can be done about it. A strong Christian will face life in such a way that selfishness will be uprooted and wrong will eventually be righted.

HYMN: "This Is My Father's World."

POEM:

> The little cares that fretted me
>   I lost them yesterday,
> Among the fields, above the sea,
>   Among the winds at play,
> Among the lowing of the herds,
>   The rustling of the trees,
> Among the singing of the birds,
>   The humming of the bees.
>
> The foolish fears of what might happen,
>   I cast them all away

HYMNS

> Among the clover-scented grass,
> Among the new-mown hay,
> Among the husking of the corn,
> Where the drowsy poppies nod,
> Where ill thoughts die and good are born—
> Out in the fields with God.
>
> —AUTHOR UNKNOWN

LITANY OF SUPPLICATION:

Leader: O thou Creator of all things, grant that our eyes that have seen the beauty of thy creation may have a clearer idea of thee.

Group: Grant us this vision, O Lord.

Leader: Since our hearts have been warmed by the beauty about us, may we bring to thee worship that is acceptable.

Group: Help us to obtain this blessing, O Lord.

Leader: Grant that our ears that have been closed to the clamor and strife about us may be opened to hear thy music.

Group: Help us to obtain this blessing, O Lord.

Leader: Grant that our tongues that have sung thy praise may now speak thy truth.

Group: Help us to obtain this blessing, O Lord.

Leader: Grant that our feet that have walked in willful ways may now walk in the paths of righteousness.

Group: Help us to obtain this blessing, O Lord.

Leader: Give unto us a clearer idea of ways in which we can uproot selfishness and conquer evil and do our part toward making this truly our Father's world.

Group: Lord, hear our prayer, and help to obtain this blessing. In Jesus' name. AMEN.

HYMN: "God, That Madest Earth and Heaven," or
"Day is Dying in the West."

BENEDICTION:

> Day is done, gone the sun,
> From the lake, from the hills, from the sky,
> Safely rest, all is well, God is nigh. AMEN.[5]

APPENDIX

NOTES

SERVICE 1, THE NAZARENE

1. By St. Augustine.
2. Isa. 57:15; I John 3:2, 3; I Cor. 13:12; lines from "The Higher Pantheism," by Alfred Tennyson.
3. "The Master's Face," by William Hurd Hillyer, from *Songs of the Steel Age,* published by Richard G. Badger & Co. Used by permission of William Hurd Hillyer.
4. From information furnished with the painting by E. C. Sherburne, art critic, and Charles Haddon Bloom.
5. Hymn by Henry S. Ninde.

SERVICE 2, CHRIST WITH MARY AND MARTHA

1. Luke 10:38-42.
2. "The Great Companion," from *Pass on the Torch,* published by Pilgrim Press. Used by permission of Allen Eastman Cross. Tune "Eudoxia."
3. Adapted from *The Gospel in Art,* by Albert Edward Bailey, published by Pilgrim Press. Used by permission of Albert Edward Bailey.
4. "The Choice," published in the *Nashville Christian Advocate.* Used by permission of Effie Smith Ely.

SERVICE 3, THE FRIEND OF THE HUMBLE

1. Matt. 5:3-6; Ps. 37:3-5, 23-25, 37.
2. From *The Book of Common Prayer.*
3. "Song of Christian Workingmen." Used by permission of James T. White & Co., publishers.
4. From *The Gospel Message in Great Pictures,* by James Carter Used by permission of Funk and Wagnalls Co., publishers.

5. "Grace in Living," published in the *Church School Magazine*. Used by permission of Edith Kent Battle.
6. From *The Book of Common Prayer*.

SERVICE 4, DEATH THE VICTOR

1. Matt. 5:9, 39, 44; 7:12; Rom. 12:17, 20, 21.
2. "A Prayer for Peace," published in the *Nashville Christian Advocate*. Used by permission of Effie Smith Ely.
3. Isa. 2:4.
4. From "Bulliet's Artless Comment," in the *Chicago Daily News* Used by permission.
5. "Peace." Used by permission of John Oxenham.

SERVICE 5, CHRIST IN GETHSEMANE

1. Based on Isa. 53.
2. Matt. 26:39.
3. From *Pictures That Preach*, by Charles Nelson Pace, Copyright 1924. Used by permission of The Abingdon Press, publishers.
4. From *Great Pictures as Moral Teachers*, by Henry E. Jackson. Used by permission of The John C. Winston Co., publishers.

SERVICE 6, FOR HE HAD GREAT POSSESSIONS

1. Matt. 19:16-22.
2. Used by permission of Chauncey R. Piety.
3. From *The Gospel in Art*, by Albert Edward Bailey, published by Pilgrim Press. Used by permission of Albert Edward Bailey.
4. "The Rich Young Ruler," published in the *Nashville Christian Advocate*. Used by permission of Effie Smith Ely.
5. "The Second Place," published in the *Nashville Christian Advocate*. Used by permission of Effie Smith Ely.

SERVICE 7, SIR GALAHAD

1. Ps. 15; Ps. 24:3, 4.
2. From *One Hundred Masterpieces of Painting*. Used by permission of Frederick A. Stokes Co., publishers.
3. "A Leader's Prayer." Used by permission of J. Lester Hankins.

SERVICE 8, THE MAGDALENE

1. Based on Ps. 51:1-4, 7, 10, 12, 15-17.
2. From *The Book of Common Prayer*.

3. Ps. 34:4; 32:1, 2.
4. Adapted from *The Gospel in Art,* by Albert Edward Bailey, published by Pilgrim Press. Used by permission of Albert Edward Bailey.
5. From *Great Pictures as Moral Teachers,* by Henry E. Jackson. Used by permission of The John C. Winston Co., publishers.

SERVICE 9, THE LOST SHEEP

1. Tune, "Carter." May be sung to "Evening Prayer."
2. John 10:9, 10, 14-16; Luke 15:4-6; Matt. 9:36; 10:1, 6, 7.
3. Adapted from *The Gospel in Art,* by Albert Edward Bailey, published by Pilgrim Press. Used by permission of Albert Edward Bailey.
4. Slightly altered. Tune "Dix"; alternate tune "Redhead No. 76."

SERVICE 10, THE HOPE OF THE WORLD

1. Ps. 24:7-10, and from *The Book of Common Prayer.*
2. Luke 18:15, 16.
3. From *The Gospel in Art* by Albert Edward Bailey, published by Pilgrim Press. Used by permission of Albert Edward Bailey.
4. "Brotherhood." Used by permission of William L. Stidger.

SERVICE 11, THE HEALER

1. Matt. 28:19, 20; II Pet. 3:9; Luke 19:10; hymn by Samuel Wolcott— tune "Kirby Bedon" or "Italian Hymn."
2. Reproduced by permission of the London Missionary Society. Copyright.
3. Adapted from Albert Schweitzer's *African Notebook.* Used by permission of the publishers, Henry Holt & Co.
4. Used by permission of Mrs. Robt. F. Jefferys.

SERVICE 12, THE PRESENCE

1. Based on Ps. 139:1-12, 17, 18.
2. From *The Book of Common Prayer.*
3. Tune "Hesperus." Used by permission of Earl Marlatt.
4. Matt. 7:7.
5. "The Secret," from *Spiritual Hilltops.* Copyright 1932. Used by permission of The Abingdon Press.

APPENDIX

SERVICE 13, THE LIGHT OF THE WORLD

1. From *The Book of Common Prayer*.
2. John 1:1-16.

SERVICE 14, THE HAND OF GOD

1. Isa. 6:3; I Chron. 16:27, 29; Ps. 34:3; Rev. 15:3; Ps. 8:1; 95:6.
2. Gen. 1:1-3, 26-28, 31.
3. From *I Saw God Wash the World,* published by The Rodeheaver-Hall-Mack Co. Used by permission of William L. Stidger.
4. Adapted from *The Life and Work of Auguste Rodin,* by Frederick Lawton. Used by permission of Charles Scribner's Sons, publishers.
5. "Our God is a Great God," published in the *Nashville Christian Advocate.* Used by permission of Robert E. Goodrich.

SERVICE 15, MOSES

1. Ps. 102:12, 25-28; 90:1, 2, 4, 9, 12, 17.
2. From *The Book of Common Prayer*.
3. Exod. 32:7, 8, 15, 19.
4. Exod. 20:3, 4.
5. Used by permission of William L. Stidger.
6. From "Prayer," by John Drinkwater. Used by permission of and by arrangement with the authorized publishers, Houghton Mifflin Co.

SERVICE 16, FRANCIS ASBURY

1. Ps. 1.
2. "Sculptor of the Soul," from *Songs from the Slums,* by Toyohiko Kagawa. Copyright 1935. Used by permission of Cokesbury Press, publishers.
3. Tune "Conisborough"; alternate tunes "Ellers" and "Morecambe."
4. "The Lure of the Unattained," published in the *International Journal of Religious Education,* February, 1930. Used by permission.

SERVICE 17, MARGARET OF NEW ORLEANS

1. From Tolstoy's "Confession of Faith."
2. Used by permission of Chauncey R. Piety.
3. Rom. 12:1, 2.
4. By St. Augustine.

NOTES

SERVICE 18, ABRAHAM LINCOLN

1. From *The Book of Common Prayer*.
2. Used by permission of Dorothy Tarrant.
3. From Lincoln's "Gettysburg Address," the Declaration of Independence, Lincoln's "Second Inaugural Address," and Henry Ward Beecher.
4. "The Master," by Thomas Curtis Clark. Used by permission of James T. White & Co., publishers.
5. "Are There No Foes?" published in *The Young People's Journal*. Used by permission of David C. Cook Publishing Co.

SERVICE 19, THE PIONEER MOTHER

1. Heb. 11:1-3, 8-10, 13-16.
2. "Pioneers! O Pioneers," from *Leaves of Grass*. Copyright, 1924, by Doubleday, Doran & Co.
3. From *A Lantern in Her Hand,* by Bess Streeter Aldrich. Used by permission of the publishers, D. Appleton-Century Co.
4. "Pioneers," published in the *Christian Home*. Used by permission of Edith Kent Battle.

SERVICE 20, THE SCOUT

1. By Isabel Crawford. Used by permission.
2. John 15:9-13.
3. "Impartiality." Used by permission of Chauncey R. Piety.

SERVICE 21, CHRIST OF THE ANDES

1. Ps. 67.
2. Tune "Duke Street."
3. Mic. 4:1, 2; Ezek. 34:25, 30; Isa. 60:1-3, 11, 12, 17, 18.
4. "Peace Hymn," published in the *Nashville Christian Advocate*. Used by permission of Effie Smith Ely.

SERVICE 22, O LOVE THAT WILL NOT LET ME GO

1. Used by permission of the National Board, Y. W. C. A.
2. I John 4:16; Ps. 37:5; Prov. 3:6; and lines from "In Memoriam," by Alfred Tennyson.
3. "Love Lives." Used by permission of William L. Stidger.
4. From *The Life of George Matheson,* by D. Macmillan.

5. "Forever," published in *Religious Telescope*. Used by permission of Effie Smith Ely.
6. Adapted from a prayer by St. Francis.

SERVICE 23, DEAR LORD AND FATHER OF MANKIND

1. Ps. 121:1-8; 91:1; 62:5.
2. By Augusta Blake Bevis. Used by permission.
3. From "The Brewing of Soma." Used by permission of and by arrangement with the authorized publishers, Houghton Mifflin Co.
4. From *A Book of Prayers for Youth,* by J. S. Hoyland. Used by permission of the publishers, Association Press.
5. Used by permission of William L. Stidger.

SERVICE 24, O GOD, OUR HELP IN AGES PAST

1. From Ps. 84, Scottish Psalter.
2. Pss. 46:1-3, 7; 31:1-3, 5, 7, 15, 16, 19, 20, 24.
3. From *The Book of Common Prayer*.
4. Ps. 90:1-6; hymn by Isaac Watts, tune "St. Anne."

SERVICE 25, WHERE CROSS THE CROWDED WAYS OF LIFE

1. By Louis F. Benson. Used by permission of Mrs. Robt. F. Jefferys.
2. Gal. 6:2, 9, 10; Matt. 11:28; hymn by Ozora S. Davis.
3. "That Our Eyes May Be Opened," published in the *Christian Home*. Used by permission of Edith Kent Battle.
4. Matt. 9:36; Luke 19:41; Matt. 23:37.
5. From *Stories of Hymns We Love,* by Cecilia M. Rudin. Used by permission of John Rudin & Co., publishers.
6. "Master of the Multitude." Used by permission of Chauncey R. Piety.

SERVICE 26, ALL CREATURES OF OUR GOD AND KING

1. Ps. 97:1; 126:3; 30:5; Eccles. 3:11; hymn by Louis F. Benson. Used by permission of Mrs. Robt. F. Jefferys.
2. "The Vespers of a Tree." Used by permission of William L. Stidger.

SERVICE 27, IN CHRIST THERE IS NO EAST OR WEST

1. Psalm 100.
2. Acts 10:34, 35; Eph. 2:14, 18, 19; hymn by Ozora S. Davis.
3. By Louis F. Benson. Used by permission of Mrs. Robt. F. Jefferys.

4. "Building God's Kingdom." Used by permission of Chauncey R. Piety.
5. From *Bees in Amber*. Used by permission of John Oxenham.
6. From *Prayers of the Social Awakening,* by Walter Rauschenbusch. Copyright, The Pilgrim Press. Used by permission.
7. "My Prayer." Used by permission of S. Ralph Harlow.
8. From *A Book of Prayers for Youth,* by J. S. Hoyland. Used by permission of the publishers, Association Press.

SERVICE 28, O YOUNG AND FEARLESS PROPHET

1. Phil. 2:5-11, 13.
2. By Louis F. Benson. Used by permission of Mrs. Robt. F. Jefferys.
3. Altered. Author unknown.
4. Used by permission of S. Ralph Harlow.

SERVICE 29, LIFT EVERY VOICE AND SING

1. Copyright, Cornhill Publishing Company. Used by permission.
2. I John 1:8, 9; Ps. 103:10-12; Matt. 18:21, 22.
3. "At the Closed Gate of Justice," published in the *Century Magazine,* June, 1913. Used by permission of D. Appleton-Century Co., copyright owners.
4. "Lift Every Voice and Sing," from *Saint Peter Relates an Incident,* by James Weldon Johnson. Copyright 1917, 1921, 1935 by James Weldon Johnson. By permission of The Viking Press, Inc., New York. Sheet music of this hymn may be obtained from Theodore Presser Music Co., 1712 Chestnut St., Philadelphia, Penn.
5. From *A Book of Prayers for Youth,* by J. S. Hoyland. Used by permission of the publishers, Association Press.

SERVICE 30, RISE UP, O MEN OF GOD

1. Acts 2:17, Heb. 8:11; Luke 13:29; Matt. 18:14; hymn by John Greenleaf Whittier.
2. "The House of Brotherhood," from *Pass on The Torch,* published by Pilgrim Press. Used by permission of Allen Eastman Cross. Tune "Materna" or "St. Michel's."
3. I Cor. 16:13.
4. Used by permission of *The Presbyterian Tribune.*
5. Used by permission of S. Ralph Harlow. Tune "Gabriel," or "Serenity" doubled.

SERVICE 31, GOD OF GRACE AND GOD OF GLORY

1. Mark 12:29-31; John 13:34.
2. From *Hymn Interpretations,* by Chas. C. Washburn. Copyright 1938. Used by permission of Cokesbury Press, publishers.
3. Prov. 3:13, 15; Ps. 119:1, 2, 11, 33, 34; Prov. 3:5, 6; Ps. 40:8, 10. Hymn used by permission of Harry Emerson Fosdick.

SERVICE 32, SILENT NIGHT

1. Luke 2:8-16.
2. Adapted from *1001 Christmas Facts and Fancies,* by Alfred C. Hottes, by permission of A. T. De La Mare Co., publishers.
3. From *The Girl's Every Day Book.* Used by permission of The Woman's Press, publishers.
4. From *Ceremonials of Common Days,* by Abbie Graham. Used by permission of The Woman's Press, publishers.
5. "The Shepherds' Vision," published in *The Independent.* Used by permission of Effie Smith Ely.

SERVICE 33, AMERICA THE BEAUTIFUL

1. Tune "Wentworth" or "Fowler."
2. Amos 4:13; 5:8; I Chron. 29:11, 14.
3. "We Thank Thee." Used by permission of James T. White & Co., publishers.
4. Ps. 33:12; Prov. 14:34; Lev. 25:10; Isa. 58:6; 26:2; Acts 17:26; Mic. 4:3.
5. "My America." Used by permission of James T. White & Co., publishers.
6. From *A Book of Prayers for Youth,* by J. S. Hoyland. Used by permission of Association Press, publishers.

SERVICE 34, CHRIST THE LORD IS RISEN TODAY

1. From *The Book of Common Prayer.*
2. Matt. 28:1-8.
3. Adapted from *Stories of Hymns We Love,* by Cecilia M. Rudin. Used by permission of John Rudin & Co., publishers.
4. "Easter," published in the *Nashville Christian Advocate.* Used by permission of Effie Smith Ely.

SERVICE 35, MARCHING WITH THE HEROES

1. Deut. 31:6; Ps. 28:7; I Cor. 16:13; Isa. 50:7; Ps. 118:14; Isa. 40:30, 31.
2. Heb. 11:32-40.
3. "The Hall of Heroes," by an author who prefers to remain unknown. Published in *Christ and the Fine Arts,* by Cynthia Pearl Maus, Harper & Bros.
4. Used by permission of Dorothy Tarrant.

SERVICE 36, I WOULD BE TRUE

1. Heb. 12:1, 2; Matt. 5:16; 7:12; 6:33; anonymous hymn.
2. "A Psalm of the Son of Man," from *Pass on the Torch,* published by Pilgrim Press. Used by permission of Allen Eastman Cross. If this is sung as a solo with quiet music, it will be more effective. Tune "Son of Man."
3. Phil. 4:8.

SERVICE 37, THIS IS MY FATHER'S WORLD

1. If this service is held out-of-doors, the hymn tune may be hummed by a choir, or a violin may be used.
2. Tune "Vesper Hymn."
3. Ps. 8:3-9.
4. From *I Saw God Wash the World,* published by The Rodeheaver-Hall-Mack Company. Used by permission of William L. Stidger.
5. Tune "Taps."

SOURCES FOR PRINTS

Printed reproductions in color of most of the paintings, as well as pictures of some of the works of sculpture, may be obtained in sizes suitable for use in worship programs from various denominational supply houses and local art stores. Of the remainder photographs are available which should prove satisfactory. The pictures marked with an asterisk (*) are likely to be difficult to find except through the source given.

Colored slides of some paintings for projection on a screen may be obtained from many denominational supply houses or from Art Education, Inc., or Gramstorff Brothers.

Addresses of the art companies and photographers mentioned are listed alphabetically below.

THE NAZARENE by Henry Stanley Todd
Master Art Reproductions

CHRIST WITH MARY AND MARTHA by Hendrik Siemiradski
Gramstorff Brothers

THE FRIEND OF THE HUMBLE by Leon Augustin L'hermitte
Gramstorff Brothers

*DEATH THE VICTOR by Robert Lindneux
Gramstorff Brothers

CHRIST IN GETHSEMANE by Heinrich Hofmann
Art Education, Inc.
Gramstorff Brothers
The House of Art
W. A. Wilde Co.

FOR HE HAD GREAT POSSESSIONS by George Frederick Watts
The House of Art

SIR GALAHAD by George Frederick Watts
Artext Prints
Art Education, Inc.
Brown-Robertson Co.
Gramstorff Brothers
The House of Art
F. A. Owen Publishing Co.
Perry Pictures

THE MAGDALENE (with cross) by Correggio
Gramstorff Brothers

THE LOST SHEEP by Alfred Soord
Art Education, Inc.
Gramstorff Brothers
The House of Art

THE HOPE OF THE WORLD by Harold Copping
William H. Dietz

THE HEALER by Harold Copping
William H. Dietz

THE PRESENCE by A. E. Borthwick
The House of Art

THE LIGHT OF THE WORLD by Holman Hunt
Art Education, Inc.
Art Education Press
Artext Prints
Brown-Robertson Co.
Campbell Prints
Gramstorff Brothers
The House of Art
Master Art Reproductions
Perry Pictures
Reinthal and Newman
W. A. Wilde Co.

THE HAND OF GOD by Auguste Rodin
Metropolitan Museum of Art

MOSES by Michelangelo
Gramstorff Brothers

*FRANCIS ASBURY by H. A. Lukeman
Dewitt Ward

*MARGARET OF NEW ORLEANS by Alexander Doyle
Charles L. Franck

ABRAHAM LINCOLN by Augustus Saint-Gaudens
Gramstorff Brothers

SOURCES FOR PRINTS

*THE PIONEER MOTHER by Alexander Proctor
   Photographic View Co.

*THE SCOUT by Cyrus Edwin Dallin
   Photographic View Co.

CHRIST OF THE ANDES
   Art Education, Inc.
   Gramstorff Brothers

ADDRESSES OF ART COMPANIES

ART EDUCATION, INC., 35 West 34th St., New York, N. Y.
ART EDUCATION PRESS, 424 Madison Ave., New York, N. Y.
ARTEXT PRINTS, Westport, Conn.
BROWN-ROBERTSON CO., 35 West 34th St., New York, N. Y.
CAMPBELL PRINTS, INC., 33 West 34th St., New York, N. Y.
WILLIAM H. DIETZ, 10 South Wabash Ave., Chicago, Ill.
CHARLES L. FRANCK, 409 Baronne St., New Orleans, La.
GRAMSTORFF BROTHERS, INC., 101-103 Ferry St., Malden, Mass.
THE HOUSE OF ART, 33 West 34th St., New York, N. Y.
MASTER ART REPRODUCTIONS, 200 Fifth Ave., New York, N. Y.
METROPOLITAN MUSEUM OF ART, New York, N. Y.
F. A. OWEN PUBLISHING CO., Danville, N. Y.
PERRY PICTURES, Malden, Mass.
PHOTOGRAPHIC VIEW CO., 606 Ridge Building, Kansas City, Mo.
REINTHAL & NEWMAN, 33 West 34th St., New York, N. Y.
DEWITT WARD, 227 West 13th St., New York City
W. A. WILDE, 131 Clarendon St., Boston, Mass.

SOURCES FOR HYMNS

Come, Peace of God
M—510.

Come Thou Almighty King
A—38; B—4; C—164; D—24;
E—354; H—52; I—1; M—2; P—
10; T—3; W—9.

Dare to Be Brave
B—320.

Day Is Dying in the West
A—17; B—87; D—12; E—96; H—
39; I—32; M—44; P—66; T—463;
W—116.

Dear Lord and Father of Mankind
A—152; B—401; D—236; E—80;
H—302; I—29; M—342; P—224;
T—242; W—79.

Fairest Lord Jesus
A—137; B—211; D—136; E—58;
H—194; I—80; M—111; P—465;
T—72; W—170.

Faith of Our Fathers
A—137; B—201; D—203; E—109;
H—267; I—13; M—256; P—220;
T—210; W—86.

Father of Lights
A—1; E—21.

For the Beauty of the Earth
A—46; B—246; C—292; D—55;
E—357; H—71; I—100; M—18;
P—168; T—16; W—105.

Forward Through the Ages
A—263; B—419; D—350; E—113;
P—400.

From All That Dwell Below the
Skies
C—293; H—388; I—200; M—17;
P—18.

From Homes of Quiet Peace
A—315; D—265.

Gather Us In
A—300; E—261; I—339; P—376.

Give Me Thy Heart
W—129.

Glorious Things of Thee Are Spo-
ken
C—197; D—247; I—35; M—382;
P—376; T—352.

God of Grace and God of Glory
M—279; W—235.

God of Our Fathers
A—273; B—224; C—493; D—302;
E—283; H—414; I—103; M—496;
P—356; T—342.

God of the Strong
A—212; E—217; M—457.

God of the Nations, Hear Our Call
D—354; I—378.

God of the Nations, Near and Far
A—296; D—323; P—380.

God's Trumpet Wakes the Slumbering World
A—203; E—146; M—262; P—260.

God That Madest Earth and Heav-
en
D—20; E—306; H—41; M—43;
P—67; W—115.

God Who Touchest Earth with
Beauty
A—223; D—222.

Go Labor On
H—376; M—292; P—330.

Gracious Spirit
D—149; H—214; I—159; P—186.

Great Master, Touch Us
A—222.

I Gave My Life for Thee
B—222; T—163.

I Would Be True
A—177; B—368; D—225; E—180;
I—158; P—469; W—184.

Immortal Love, Forever Full
A—140; E—68; H—178; I—56;
P—27; T—84.

APPENDIX

In Christ There Is No East or West
A—299; D—314; E—273; H—341;
I—235; M—507; P—389; T—375;
W—166.

In Life's Earnest Morning
A—213; E—139.

In the Hour of Trial
B—467; C—391; D—229; E—104;
H—255; I—91; M—274; P—242;
T—238; W—39.

Into the Woods My Master Went
A—119; B—420; D—121; E—841-
247; M—132; P—126; T—99;
W—210.

Jesus Calls Us O'er the Tumult
A—144; B—159; D—168; E—106;
H—223; I—28; M—233; P—152;
T—284; W—49.

Jesus, Kneel Beside Me
E—107; H—494; M—308.

Jesus Shall Reign
A—305; B—150; C—219; D—310;
E—380; H—377; I—21; M—479;
P—373; T—392; W—13.

Jesus, the Very Thought of Thee
A—158; B—206; C—353; D—197;
E—358; H—309; I—112; M—348;
P—150; T—76.

Joyful, Joyful, We Adore Thee
A—43; D—48; E—49; H—5; I—
306; M—12; T—25.

Just As I Am, Thine Own to Be
A—145; B—411; D—181; E—136;
I—63; P—428; T—280; W—183.

Lead On, O King Eternal
A—199; B—236; D—208; E—177;
H—371; M—278; P—251; T—301;
W—21.

Life of Ages, Richly Poured
A—214; E—190; H—95; M—405.

Lift Up Our Hearts
A—295; H—405; M—472.

Lord, for Tomorrow and Its Needs
A—317; I—161; M—314; T—360;
W—102.

Lord, Speak to Me
A—251; C—212; D—293; E—216;
H—399; I—67; M—460; P—339;
T—379; W—167.

Love Divine, All Loves Excelling
A—67; B—19; C—276; D—231;
E—356; H—308; I—8; M—372;
T—21; W—22.

Love Thyself Last
A—239; D—276.

March On, O Soul, with Strength
A—184; D—220; E—110; H—273;
M—264; P—274; T—30.

'Mid All the Traffic of the Ways
A—159; H—322; M—341; T—237.

Marching with the Heroes
A—259; D—213; E—112; T—298;
W—162.

More Like the Master
W—60.

Must Jesus Bear the Cross Alone?
B—152; I—170; M—276; T—416;
W—56.

My Country, 'Tis of Thee
A—279; B—468; C—490; D—304;
E—293; H—412; I—17; M-489;
P—345; T—338; W—226.

My God, I Thank Thee
A—51; D—361; E—204; H—73;
I—122; M—9; P—11.

My Soul, Be on Thy Guard
B—247; C—272; E—378; I—79;
M—277; P—256; T—295.

Now in the Days of Youth
A—146; D—175; P—477.

Now on Land and Sea Descending
M—45; P—57; T—462; W—178.

Now Thank We All Our God
A—325; C—283; D—358; E—303; H—459; I—191; M—7; P—12.

O Beautiful, for Spacious Skies
A—271; B—39; D—297; E—282; H—411; I—39; M—491; P—350; T—339; W—228.

O Brother Man, Fold to Thy Heart
A—244; B—403; D—283; E—258; H—403; M—466; P—310; W—172.

O for a Closer Walk with God
H—259; I—95; M—228; P—199; T—256; W—26.

O God, Beneath Thy Guiding Hand
A—270; D—257; E—116; H—462; I—93; M—493; P—347.

O God, Our Help in Ages Past
B—435; M—533; P—177; W—196.

O Grant Us Light
H—210; I—355; T—44.

O Jesus Master, when Today
E—212; I—359; M—470; P—307; T—278.

O Jesus, Thou Art Standing
A—148; B—242; C—322; D—174; E—375; H—228; I—77; M—197; P—246; T—170; W—132.

O Jesus, Youth of Nazareth
A—103.

O Little Town of Bethlehem
A—82; B—144; C—31; D—78; E—330; H—121; I—26; M—100; P—74; T—55; W—214.

O Love That Wilt Not Let Me Go
A—154; B—231; C—343; D—196; E—37; I—38; M—318; P—289; T—26; W—211.

O Master, Let Me Walk with Thee
A—197; B—202; D—182; E—214; I—12; M—259; P—291; T—271; W—50.

O Master Workman of the Race
A—98; D—106; E—74; H—140; M—118; P—328; T—82; W—58.

Once to Every Man and Nation
D—184; E—240; H—373; M—263; P—326.

O Son of Man, Thou Madest Known
A—188; D—207; E—175; M—121; P—329.

O Worship the King
A—36; B—2; C—294; D—29; E—59; H—2; I—15; M—4; P—5; T—7; W—7.

O Young and Fearless Prophet
M—266; W—179.

O Zion, Haste
A—306; B—151; C—224; D—308; E—270; H—382; I—145; M—475; P—372; T—395; W—16.

Praise, My Soul, the King of Heaven
C—289; H—14; I—312; M—77; T—6.

Praise the Lord
A—30; C—300; D—26; H—10; I—254; M—11; P—7; T—10.

Purer Yet Purer
I—129; T—260.

Rejoice, the Lord Is King
C—126; D—137; E—346; H—193; I—420; M—171.

Rise Up, O Men of God
A—254; B—186; D—288; E—224; H—401; I—292; M—267; P—313; T—274; W—147.

Saviour, Like a Shepherd Lead Us
B—13; C—565; H—458; I—137; M—337; P—492; T—323; W—69.

Saviour, Thy Dying Love
D—198; H—396; I—155; M—219; P—486; T—273; W—33.

Silent Night
A—81; B—146; C—530; D—83;
E—302; H—132; I—72; M—106;
P—98; T—60; W—212.

Still, Still with Thee
A—6; E—20; H—107; I—115;
M—40; P—50; T—454; W—114.

Strong Son of God, Immortal Love
A—215; D—188; E—70; H—175;
I—188; M—206; P—153.

Sun of My Soul, Thou Saviour Dear
A—215; B—177; C—463; D—113;
E—93; H—37; I—64; M—56;
P—61; T—457; W—204.

The Land We Love Is Calling
A—276; E—279.

The Light of God Is Falling
D—279; H—400; M—468; P—309;
T—376.

The Lord Is My Shepherd
A—57; B—22; C—255; D—70;
E—365; H—97; I—197; M—70;
P—283; T—34.

There's a Song in the Air
A—84; M—98; P—82; W—216.

There's a Stranger
B—29.

There Were Ninety and Nine
B—36; M—247.

These Things Shall Be
A—293; E—189; H—423; I—276;
M—512; P—378.

The Spacious Firmament on High
D—53; H—69; I—144; M—66;
P—160; T—8.

The Voice of God Is Calling
E—235; M—454; P—337; W—168.

This Is My Father's World
A—39; D—52; E—51; H—70;
I—226; M—72; P—464; T—332;
W—106.

'Tis Midnight, and on Olive's Brow
I—143; M—133; P—119; T—96.

True-hearted, Whole-hearted
I—104; M—255; W—66.

To the Knights in the Days of Old
A—230; D—219; E—147; I—379;
W—182.

We Thank Thee, Lord, Thy Paths
A—249; B—301; D—287; E—223;
H—367; I—456; M—458; P—340.

We've a Story to Tell to the Nations
A—302; B—379; D—306; I—121;
M—501; P—374; W—158.

When I Survey the Wondrous Cross
A—123; B—191; C—97; D—118;
E—376; H—152; I—60; M—148;
P—122; T—88; W—32.

Where Cross the Crowded Ways of Life
A—265; B—405; C—235; D—68;
E—60; H—410; I—61; M—465;
P—140; T—330; W—195.

Work, for the Night Is Coming
B—243; I—109; M—293; P—502;
W—201.

Ye Fair Green Hills of Galilee
A—102; D—100; M—124.

Young and Radiant He is Standing
A—99.